One World KITCHEN

— THE —

COOKBOOK

TouchWood
Editions

The information in this book is true and complete to the best of the author's
knowledge. All recommendations are made without guarantee on the part
of the author or TouchWood Editions. The author and publisher disclaim
any liability in connection with the use of this information.

HOST PHOTOGRAPHY: © Katia Pershin
FOOD PHOTOGRAPHY: Stephanie Brown, Kathy McIntyre
POST-PRODUCTION PHOTOGRAPHY: Madeline Charlton
COVER DESIGN: Page & Design
INTERIOR DESIGN: Page & Design
INTERIOR TYPESETTING: Pete Kohut

Printed in China

LIBRARY AND ARCHIVES CANADA CATALOGUING IN PUBLICATION
Knight, Chris, 1960–, author
      One world kitchen: the cookbook / Chris Knight.

Companion cookbook to Gusto TV series One world kitchen.
Issued in print and electronic formats.
ISBN 978-1-77151-141-4

      1. International cooking. 2. One world kitchen (Television program).
3. Cookbooks. I. Title.

TX725.A1K59 2015   641.59   C2015-904133-3

Canadian   Patrimoine
Heritage   canadien
The publisher acknowledges the financial support of the Government
of Canada through the Canada Book Fund (CBF) and the Province of
British Columbia through the Book Publishing Tax Credit.

15 16 17 18 19   5 4 3 2 1

This book was produced using FSC®-certified, acid-free papers,
processed chlorine free, and printed with soya-based inks.

To Taryn. Love this book. Love you more. Thanks for putting up with me.

Contents

INTRODUCTION

Welcome to *One World Kitchen*. When we launched Gusto TV in 2013, we knew we had our work cut out for us. Taking on a well-established mega-corporate competitor living off a slick American programming feed was a tall order. In fact, a lot of sage and learned TV types thought we were off our collective nut. The truth is, we probably were a bunch of loons. Television is a global multi-million-dollar business and no place for a tiny private start-up not working out of Torontosaurus Rex. I suppose there is something to be said for not knowing any better.

Anyway, we "lit up" on December 11, 2013 (11-12-13) at 7:00 PM. Our very first show was the very first episode of television Julia Child ever made: a beautiful piece of fun, honest, unsophisticated, black-and-white performance art. And we ran it commercial-free. This was our shout-out to the world that we were different—a food and cooking channel actually run by people who love food and cooking! Within six weeks of launching, our ratings rocked, the viewer mail began to pour in, and we've never looked back.

TV networks are (not surprisingly) defined by the shows they air. Some are very focused (you won't see *The Good Wife* on a sports channel, for instance) while others are a mish-mash of programming genres, depending on the time of day you're watching. TV programs are commodities bought and sold all over the world (our shows, for instance, have been on in 170 countries). Gusto TV is all about food. Not contests or game shows. Not guys with big hair eating hamburgers the size of their head. We are real people. Cooking. Real food. And what's more, we're unabashedly proud to be Canadian.

Three months into broadcast, we sat around and agonized over what was going to be Gusto's first original production. What would be the first show we'd produce ourselves to show our viewers that we were different?

We think Canada is the most culturally diverse country in the world. Successive generations of enlightened immigration policy have made us unique and diverse and indisputably the best place to live. Practically every nation's favored son or daughter has found a home here. So, we asked

ourselves, why isn't that cultural diversity reflected in food television? Go into your local grocery store and you'll likely find a sushi counter or Thai chicken or Greek salad or curried lentil soup. Canadians have sophisticated, inquisitive palates. So why was food TV all burgers and deep fried?

The answer was *One World Kitchen*—a television series that celebrates global cuisine as interpreted here at home in Canada. But which cuisines? And who would we get to be the new faces of Gusto? And so the adventure began.

In February of 2014, we set off on a cross-country journey to find chefs and cooks and food lovers who could share their passion for their cuisines. We held auditions from Montreal to Vancouver. Then we went back and did it again and again, always searching for fresh, new faces that would help us re-invent food and cooking on television (and the internet—we're all over the internet).

We met so many wonderful, joyous people. But it takes a very special person to be a food TV star. We take you out of your life and plop you in a studio surrounded by strangers. We ask you to always be "natural" and fun and celebratory during a crazy roller-coaster sixteen-hour day. Oh, and by the way, you have the small burden of representing an entire cuisine, an entire culture, while you're at it. And the camera never blinks. It captures everything. We digitize your soul and chop you up into little bits and assemble you into a show and bounce you off a satellite or run you down a cable into the homes of people you will never ever meet. And somehow, through all of this, you have to be able to make an immediate emotional connection with folks who want to relax and be entertained at the end of a long day. Tough gig.

And boy, did we luck out. We found Hana, Natalia, Pailin, Vijaya, and Vanessa—five extraordinary women from five very different backgrounds, each passionate and articulate and amazing in their own way. What you may not understand (if you haven't seen the show) is how remarkable it is that these five women came together in this one place at this one time to create what might be the best cooking show ever. Not because of the set or the music or the camera angles. It's because they are honest and real.

These women are experts in their particular cuisines, with deep cultural knowledge bursting from within each one of them. Their kindness and generosity and love are the secret ingredients in every recipe in this book. We are privileged to have worked with them; we are the simple conduit that allows them the opportunity to share.

So what do these women, these cultures, and these cuisines have in common? The techniques and ingredients are different (that's what makes this such a great cookbook). This is what we know to be true: the best-prepared meal is nothing without friends and family. In Argentina, Italy, Japan, India, and Thailand, what is most important is not the complexity of flavours or the provenance of ingredients. It is the coming together at table. Sharing food makes any dish exceptional. After all, isn't that what food and cooking are all about? Sharing? No matter where you are, no matter where you come from, dinner is our common currency.

Both this book and the show the recipes come from require a tremendous amount of work from very talented people. The entire list of names would fill another page. I do want to single out Kathy McIntyre and Stephanie Browne for the exceptional photo work (all done on set while we were shooting the show), Karrie Galvin for her killer food styling, and Madeline Charlton for stylish design and Photoshop work. You wouldn't be reading this were it not for the Herculean work (and patience) of everyone at TouchWood. In particular, I'd like to thank Taryn Boyd, Grace Yaginuma, Mauve Pagé, Pete Kohut, and Renée Layberry who turned this book around in what must be a publishing-world speed record.

There will never be another show or another cookbook like this one. All of us at One World Kitchen hope that this book will inspire you and become a dog-eared, sauce-smudged, go-to favourite in your home. Enjoy!

—Chris Knight,
President and CEO of Gusto TV
Ottawa, ON

ARGENTINA

Natalia Machado

I am trying to remember the first time food meant something more to me than nourishment for the body. When did it start becoming nourishment for the soul? When did it turn into an art? And when did I become a cook?

My first memories as a little girl took place in the kitchen, whether it was my grandmother's, full of large pots of wonderful Spanish-inspired stews ready to be served at any time (which was all the time), or my mom's kitchen, her busily trying to keep up with three kids (and with at least three friends hanging around) or starting a small, then-rather-popular line of preserves with my aunt. It was like a busy restaurant kitchen, where we would be testing recipes, trying out the results, and bottling flavourful concoctions.

My father was no stranger to cooking either. Although never with a stove—his grilling skills are well known! Parrillas (Argentinian grills) are a strong part of the Argentines' culture, and as a consequence, they are a part of my identity as a cook. Open fire always calls for good cooking. To me, asados—all-day Argentinian barbecues where lots of family and friends gather together—function as a creator of great memories. My father treated the grill like he did his architectural designs, with great respect and precision from the moment he lit the charcoal to laying out the final spread of meat where every piece was meticulously sprinkled with coarse salt. He was one of the first of many cooks who inspired me to take my life by the spoon and enjoy cooking.

I started medical school right after I finished high school. Despite it being a long childhood dream of mine, it turned out medicine was not for me. I found myself at eighteen clueless as to what to do next. My mom suggested I give cooking classes a chance. I couldn't think of any good reason not to—after all, I loved cooking.

One class and I was totally hooked. Everything I learned would make me love it even more. And not only was I becoming crazy about it, I was also realizing it may actually be a way to make a living.

I started just like everybody does—an internship here, a prep gig there. Finally I worked as a pastry chef. After only two months, the chef quit in the middle of a very busy Saturday night service, and I was asked to take the lead until the company could hire someone new. Well, they never ended up

doing that. I was in charge of an incredibly busy cosmopolitan restaurant, and I loved every minute of it.

Two years later I felt like I wanted even more. Without really thinking it through, I bought a plane ticket to New York City. Although I left behind what had been a completely enriching experience, I felt that maybe something else was in store for me.

NYC meant starting from zero. I took a job as a hostess, just to be close to a kitchen. Then a part-time pastry job for which I had to commute two hours back and forth. It was then that I met a woman named Maricel Presilla, a talented and inspiring Cuban chef who took me in and taught me everything she knew. She opened her home and her restaurant to me and allowed me to work first on her cookbook and later as her sous chef. My cooking went up to a whole different level. I am immensely grateful to her.

After working with Maricel for more than three years, I was offered the opportunity to run my own kitchen: Industria Argentina opened in Tribeca in 2005. It was the beginning of a love affair.

Being far away from home made me fall in love with my country's cuisine. I needed to learn more about it. And after twelve years in New York and two years in Montreal, I am still learning about Argentinian cuisine. I find myself dusting off my grandmother's recipes and featuring them on my menus and in my everyday cooking.

Argentinian cuisine is simple and straightforward. It features wholesome ingredients that translate into flavourful dishes. It contains influences from the Old World—brought in by European immigrants, mostly Italian and Spanish, who settled in Argentina during the crises of the early years of the last century—and elements from the New World, with treasures growing right on South American soil. It's food that has its own soul, capable of melting together cultures that originally had nothing to do with one another and were separated by thousands of miles.

Today, I cook for my family with the same dedication that I cook for my guests, at home and at my restaurant. I have a wonderful and supportive husband and two beautiful restless boys who fill my kitchen with laughter and love. And I cook for my family what my mom once cooked for me. My hope is that when the boys grow older, they'll remember our family dinners and the time we spent around the stove, and that these memories will stay with them forever.

Every recipe in this chapter takes me to a different place or a different moment in my life. To a Sunday afternoon waiting by the grill for the steak to be a punto (medium), to Christmas day filled with family and all of its comforting meals. This is why I chose them. They transport me to a fabulous land of great cooking, to my dearest Argentina.

I hope you enjoy cooking them as much as I do.

abrazos,
Natalia

Recipes

CHIPÁS

Makes 12 chipás

Think of this as Argentinian cheese bread, shaped as little bundles perfect for snacking on or to sop up soup or gravy—beats old-fashioned rolls any day. Tapioca starch (or tapioca flour) is made from cassava root and should be available at your grocery store or any Latin or Asian market; if you can't find it, cornstarch will substitute nicely. Friulano cheese is a firm, golden-yellow Canadian cheese that works well in these rolls; you can also use mozzarella.

1 large egg

⅔ cup (160 mL) milk

6 oz (170 g) Friulano
   cheese, grated
   (about 1 cup/250 mL)

3 Tbsp (45 mL) butter, melted

1¾ cups (435 mL)
   tapioca starch

1 cup (250 mL)
   all-purpose flour

1½ tsp (7.5 mL)
   baking powder

¼ tsp (2.5 mL) kosher salt

Preheat the oven to 350°F (180°C). Line a baking sheet with parchment paper.

In a large bowl, stir together the egg, milk, cheese, and butter. In another bowl, combine the tapioca starch, regular flour, baking powder, and salt. Sprinkle the dry ingredients into the egg mixture, stir, and then use your hands to form a rough dough.

Turn out the dough onto a lightly floured surface, and knead for 2 minutes. Form into golf ball–size pieces, and place onto the prepared baking sheet. Lightly press down to flatten.

Bake until golden brown, about 12 minutes. Transfer the chipás on a wire rack and let cool.

FAINÁ

Serves 2 (makes 6 to 8 wedges)

This flatbread is gluten free, the chickpea flour giving it a unique texture. Oddly enough, we usually serve this bread in Argentina with . . . pizza. As in, fainá served *alongside* pizza slices. Not fainá as a base for pizza toppings. And Argentinians are all pretty much all beautiful and skinny, so go figure! Feel free to try this sans pizza and dip it in a nice chimichurri sauce instead (recipes on page 40 and 47).

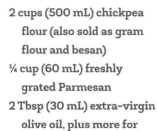

2 cups (500 mL) chickpea flour (also sold as gram flour and besan)

¼ cup (60 mL) freshly grated Parmesan

2 Tbsp (30 mL) extra-virgin olive oil, plus more for the pan

1½ cups (375 mL) water

In a bowl, whisk together the chickpea flour, Parmesan, olive oil, and water. Cover and let rest for 2 hours.

Preheat the oven to 400°F (200°C).

Heat an 8-inch (20 cm) cast iron skillet over medium-high heat. Add the oil and allow to heat for 1 minute. Quickly add the fainá batter. It will bubble up immediately. Place the pan in the oven.

Bake for about 15 minutes. To check, insert a toothpick in the centre; the fainá is done if it comes out clean.

Remove from the pan, and let rest before slicing into 6 to 8 wedges.

EMPANADAS
Makes 20 empanadas

There is likely nothing more Argentinian than the empanada. It's sold on practically every street corner, in stores and in carts, fresh and frozen, fried and baked. And they come in all manner of shapes and sizes and flavours. Empanadas can be sweet or savoury, packed with juicy meats, or vegetarian. Master the dough, and you've got a world of empanada fillings to choose from. We have two on the following pages. The secret to the dough is the lard, so don't skip it!

**7 oz (200 g) flour
(about 1⅔ cups/410 mL)**
1 tsp (5 mL) kosher salt
**1.4 oz (40 g) lard
(about 3 Tbsp/45 mL)**
**Filling for savoury meat or
fugazzeta empanadas
(page 20–21)**
**3 large egg yolks beaten with
1 Tbsp (15 mL) water, for
the egg wash**

Sift the flour and salt into a bowl, and then mix together. Using your hands, rub the lard into the dough until you have a sandy texture. Add enough ice-cold water to form the slightly stiff dough, using your hands to incorporate. Turn out to a lightly floured surface. Knead the dough for 5 to 7 minutes, or until smooth, firm, and elastic. (The dough will be very firm.)

Divide the dough into 4 equal pieces, and shape each piece into a disc, wrapping each disc individually with plastic wrap. Allow to rest for 1 hour on the counter before using. (You can also refrigerate the dough for up to 24 hours, but let it come to room temperature before using.)

Preheat the oven to 375°F (190°C). Line a baking sheet with parchment paper.

Lightly dust the work surface with flour. Roll out each disc to a ⅛-inch (3 mm) thickness, and cut out circles with a 5½-inch (14 cm) cutter. (Or you can cut out the same-size circle using parchment paper and then trace it with a paring knife.) Reroll the dough as necessary; you should have about 20 circles in the end, making 4 circles with each disc.

Using a ¼-' (60 mL) ice cream scoop or measuring cup, mound the filling in the centre of the dough leaving a ½-inch (1 cm) border. Lightly moisten the edge of the dough with a little water, and fold over into a half-moon shape and seal the edges together. Finish by making a decorative edging (see below). (The empanadas can be set aside at this point, covered in the refrigerator.)

Place the empanadas on the parchment paper–lined baking sheet. Brush lightly with the egg wash, and bake for 20 minutes, or until golden. Allow to cool for a few minutes before serving.

. . . CONTINUED

Beef Empanada

SAVOURY MEAT EMPANADA FILLING

The ground beef empanada is a true classic. Make the filling twenty-four hours before making the empanadas so that the spices have a chance to meld with the beef.

2 medium Spanish onions, finely diced

1 red bell pepper, finely diced

1 Tbsp (15 mL) extra-virgin olive oil or sunflower oil

1 lb (450 g) ground beef

1½ Tbsp (22.5 mL) ground cumin

1 Tbsp (15 mL) paprika

2 tsp (10 mL) red chili flakes

6 green onions, green parts only, finely chopped

Sauté the onion and red pepper in a large skillet in the oil over medium-low heat, until translucent and soft, about 5 minutes. Season with salt and freshly ground pepper. Remove the vegetables from the pan and set aside.

To the same pan, add a little more oil and sauté the beef over high heat. Once the meat has browned, reduce the heat to low and add the onions and red peppers back to the pan. Continue cooking for about 10 minutes, stirring occasionally.

Stir in the cumin, paprika, and chili flakes, and mix well. Let the filling rest in the fridge until chilled, ideally for 24 hours for the flavours to meld.

Stir the green onions into the mixture before assembling the empanadas.

DEEP-FRIED EMPANADAS

You can also deep-fry empanadas instead of baking them. Line a baking sheet with paper towels. In a large heavy-bottomed pot or wok, heat about 4 cups (1 L) of vegetable oil to 375°F (190°C) over medium-high heat. Deep-fry the empanadas 3 to 4 at a time, being sure not to overcrowd. Cook, turning it over once, for 4 minutes or until light golden brown and crispy. Remove from the oil and drain on the paper towels.

FUGAZZETA EMPANADA FILLING

The Danish and Swiss cheeses (havarti and raclette) here suggest there are many cultures that make up modern-day Argentina. Feel free to substitute any medium-firm cheese that will melt inside the empanada once it hits the hot oven or deep fryer.

1 Tbsp (15 mL) extra-virgin olive oil

1 large Spanish onion, cut into ¼-inch (6 mm) slices

7 oz (200 g) havarti cheese, grated

7 oz (200 g) raclette cheese, rind removed, grated

3 Tbsp (45 mL) dried oregano

2 tsp (10 mL) red chili flakes

Heat the olive oil in a skillet over medium heat. Sauté the onions for 5 minutes, then reduce the heat to medium-low and continue to cook for 10 minutes or until soft and golden. Set aside in a bowl, allowing the onions to cool.

Add the cheeses, then season with the oregano and chili flakes, and salt and freshly ground pepper to taste.

EMPANADA SHAPES

Take the half-moon empanada and seal the edges well. Then you can make the following shapes:

- *Carne*: Make a little fold at one corner, and then make the next fold over the first one. Do this about thirteen consecutive times from one end to another. This is the most classic edging.
- *Pollo*: Simply use the tines of a fork to imprint the edges.
- *Puerro*: Gather the two points together and join them while keeping the edging quite flat. It will look like a tortellini. The two points should stick together without water, but add a touch of water if it doesn't.

SWISS CHARD FRITTERS

Serves 4 as an appetizer

It's not just empanadas that are popular in Argentina! We use Swiss chard for our version of the fritter, and make our own homemade honey mustard to dip them in.

1 large bunch Swiss chard

4 large eggs, lightly beaten

⅓ cup (80 mL) milk

1½ cups (375 mL) all-purpose flour

2 tsp (10 mL) baking powder

½ cup (125 mL) freshly grated Parmesan

2 green onions, finely chopped

¼ tsp (1 mL) freshly grated nutmeg

1 tsp (5 mL) granulated sugar

Vegetable oil for deep-frying, about 4 cups (1 L)

About ½ cup (125 mL) homemade spicy mustard (page 24)

Prepare the Swiss chard by removing any discoloured leaves and separating the stems from the leaves (including up the middle of the leaf), reserving the stems for another use. Place water and a steamer basket in a large pot, and bring to a boil over high heat. Place the leaves in the steamer basket, and cover and steam for 1 minute or just until chard wilts and softens slightly. Remove from the pot, drain, and let cool completely. Roughly chop. You should have about 1 cup (250 mL).

In a medium bowl, whisk the eggs and slowly add the milk. Into a separate bowl, sift the flour and baking powder and mix to combine. Add the egg mixture to the flour and whisk to evenly incorporate.

Add the Swiss chard, then the Parmesan, green onions, nutmeg, and sugar, and season with salt and freshly ground pepper. Mix well to form a thick but fluid batter, adjusting the thickness by adding more flour or milk as needed.

Line a baking sheet with paper towels. In a medium-size heavy-bottomed pot or wok, heat the vegetable oil to 350°F (177°C) over medium-high heat, making sure the temperature doesn't go beyond 375°F (191°C). You don't want to deep-fry at too high a temperature—otherwise the fritter will brown before the interior is fully cooked.

Using either a 1-tablespoon-size (15 mL) ice cream scoop or 2 large soup spoons, drop tablespoonsful of the batter into the hot oil. Deep-fry until light golden brown, flipping the fritters over to ensure even cooking. Remove using a slotted spoon or spider and place on the paper towel–lined baking sheet.

Serve immediately while still hot and crisp with the mustard.

...CONTINUED

SPICY HONEY MUSTARD
Makes 1½ cups (375 mL)

This mustard will keep in the refrigerator for up to a month; mustard and honey are natural preservatives.

¼ cup (60 mL) yellow mustard seeds
¼ cup (60 mL) brown mustard seeds
½ cup (125 mL) white wine vinegar
¼ cup (60 mL) water
¼ cup (60 mL) honey
½ tsp (2.5 mL) kosher salt

In a spice grinder (or coffee grinder set aside for spices), process the mustard seeds until mostly broken and ground up. In a small bowl, combine the mustard seeds, vinegar, and water. Cover and let sit at room temperature for 24 hours.

Transfer the mixture into a blender, add the honey and salt, and process until smooth. If you'd like a coarser mustard, use a food processor.

SALMON CRUDO WITH CHARRED AVOCADOS AND LEMONS

Serves 6 as an appetizer

Crudo is similar to salmon sashimi, but infused with herbs and lemon zest. Chill the avocados so they don't get mushy when you grill them.

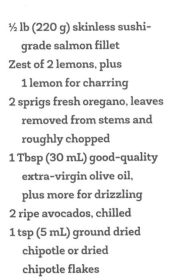

½ lb (220 g) skinless sushi-grade salmon fillet

Zest of 2 lemons, plus 1 lemon for charring

2 sprigs fresh oregano, leaves removed from stems and roughly chopped

1 Tbsp (30 mL) good-quality extra-virgin olive oil, plus more for drizzling

2 ripe avocados, chilled

1 tsp (5 mL) ground dried chipotle or dried chipotle flakes

Fleur de sel, to finish

Place the salmon in a covered nonreactive container. Sprinkle evenly with the lemon zest and chopped oregano, and drizzle with 1 tablespoon (15 mL) olive oil to coat. Cover and leave in the refrigerator to marinate for 2 hours.

When ready to serve, preheat the grill to medium-high. Halve the avocados, keeping the skin on, then remove and discard the pit, drizzle with olive oil, and season with salt and freshly ground pepper. Cut the unzested lemon into wedges, and drizzle just to coat with olive oil.

Clean and oil the grill grates to prevent sticking. Place the lemon wedges and avocado (flesh side down) on the grill, and allow to cook just until nice golden char marks develop, about 1 minute. Remove.

Cut the salmon into ¼-inch (6 mm) slices, and place on a serving platter. Carefully remove the peel from the avocado, or scoop out the flesh. Cut into about ¼-inch (6 mm) slices. Place with the salmon along with the grilled lemon wedges.

Drizzle with more olive oil, and sprinkle on the chipotle flakes and fleur de sel.

DUCK BREAST CARPACCIO WITH LEMON CURD AND SUGAR-CURED ONIONS

Serves 6 to 9 as an appetizer, and makes 1 cup (250 mL) sugar-cured onions and 1 cup (250 mL) lemon curd

The duck takes on a rich purple hue the longer it cures in the salt and sugar mix. And as a citrusy counterpoint to the sweetness of the duck, the lemon curd is brilliant. Rounding out the entire dish are the pickled onions, which provide a tart, crunchy contrast.

3 duck breasts, skin on, quills removed

3 star anise

Two 2-inch (5 cm) pieces cinnamon sticks

1 Tbsp (15 mL) black peppercorns

1 Tbsp (15 mL) coriander seeds

4 cloves

2 lbs (900 g) coarse pickling salt (about 3 cups/750 mL)

2 lbs (900 g) light brown sugar (about 2 cups/500 mL)

3 pears, unpeeled and sliced, to serve

SUGAR-CURED ONIONS

1 cup (250 mL) white wine vinegar

3 Tbsp (45 mL) brown sugar

2 red onions, thinly sliced

LEMON CURD

6 large yolks

½ cup (125 mL) fresh lemon juice, plus more to taste

¼ cup granulated sugar

3 Tbsp (45 mL) butter

Zest of 2 lemons

Pluck any remaining feathers and quills from the duck breasts, and remove excess fat and any sinew. Set aside.

In a spice grinder (or coffee grinder set aside for spices), process all of the spices—the star anise, cinnamon, peppercorns, coriander, and cloves—until almost a fine powder. In a bowl, mix the pickling salt, brown sugar, and the spices.

Spread one-third of this mixture in a shallow dish or baking sheet a little larger than the 3 duck breasts. Lay the duck on top. Use the remaining mixture to completely cover the duck. Cover with plastic wrap and refrigerate for 24 hours.

SUGAR-CURED ONIONS: Cure the onions the same day you start curing the duck. Pour the vinegar and brown sugar into a bowl or covered container, stirring to dissolve the sugar completely. Add the onions, toss to coat, and refrigerate, covered, for 24 hours.

LEMON CURD: Put all the ingredients into a medium saucepan over low heat, whisking to incorporate. Once the butter melts and the sugar dissolves, switch to a heatproof rubber spatula. Gently cook until the mixture coats the back of a spoon, about 5 minutes.

Transfer to a small bowl or container, and place plastic wrap directly onto the surface of the lemon curd to prevent a skin from forming. Allow to sit at room temperature for about 15 minutes.

The mixture will have set a bit. Whisk the curd, and add more lemon juice if it needs more acidity or the mixture is too thick. Will keep refrigerated for 5 days.

TO SERVE: Rinse the salt and sugar mixture from the duck using cold water, and pat dry with paper towels. Using a very sharp knife, cut into thin slices. Serve with the cured onions, lemon curd, and pear. (Extra portions of the breast can be frozen. Wrap tightly in several layers of plastic wrap, and freeze in resealable plastic bag.)

BURNT RICOTTA SALATA SALAD

Serves 6 as a starter or side dish

That's right, *burnt* ricotta. Charred on a super-hot skillet—known as Argentinian *chapa*-style—the cheese develops a smoky flavour and crisp texture. Use it as a topping for this simple salad featuring peppery arugula, salty olives, and juicy cherry tomatoes.

3 Tbsp (45 mL) red
wine vinegar

1 tsp (5 mL) granulated sugar

5 Tbsp (75 mL) extra-virgin
olive oil, divided

12 oz (340 g) cherry
tomatoes (about 2 cups),
cut in half

1 cup (250 mL) kalamata
or sun-dried olives

10 oz (285 g)
ricotta salata

2 green serrano chilies

3 cups (750 mL)
fresh arugula

½ tsp (2.5 mL) red chili flakes

In a small bowl, whisk together the vinegar, sugar, and 3 table-spoons (45 mL) of the olive oil. Season with salt and freshly ground pepper (but remember that the olives and ricotta salata are quite salty). Add the cherry tomatoes and toss to coat. Remove the pits from olives and cut in half. Toss the olives with the tomatoes and place on a serving platter.

Slice the ricotta salata into 2-inch (5 cm) pieces that are about ½ inch (1 cm) thick. Place in a bowl. Add the whole chilies to the ricotta, and toss with the remaining 2 tablespoons (30 mL) olive oil.

Heat a large cast iron skillet over high heat (or a chapa if you have one). Add the ricotta and chilies in batches, so they are not overcrowding the pan.

Cook for 10 seconds without moving, and as soon as you see the cheese turning a rich golden colour on the bottom, flip and cook the other side. Remove the chilies as soon as they blister and slightly char.

Roughly chop the chilies and break up the cheese. Place on the platter over the tomatoes and olives. Toss in the arugula, and sprinkle with the red chili flakes.

GRILLED FENNEL AND POTATO ENSALADA

Serves 6

This might be considered Argentinian potato salad because the ingredients are grilled. The potatoes are parboiled first, then cooked to a golden brown in a skillet. The fennel and lemon, both charred, bring a nice smokiness to the dish.

2 bulbs fennel, green
  stalks removed

15 small red baby potatoes

4 cups (1 L) chicken stock

3 Tbsp (45 mL) extra-virgin
  olive oil, divided,
  plus more for the
  charred lemon

1 lemon

2 tsp (10 mL) fresh thyme

Good-quality extra-virgin
  olive oil, for drizzling

Place the baby potatoes in a medium saucepan over medium-high heat. Add the stock and some salt and bring to a boil. Once the stock is boiling, reduce the heat to a simmer, and cook for 10 minutes or until the potatoes are al dente. Drain the potatoes. Reserve the stock for another use if desired. Allow the potatoes to cool.

On a cutting board, and using the palm of your hand, gently smash the potato into a flat round shape, keeping it intact with cracks of the potato flesh exposed.

Place a large cast iron skillet over medium-high heat. Add 2 tablespoons (30 mL) of the olive oil, and heat for 1 minute. Add the potatoes, and allow to cook until a golden caramel crust forms on one side, about 4 to 5 minutes. Flip and do the same for the other side, adjusting the heat if necessary. Remove from the pan and keep warm. Do not clean out the pan.

Preheat the grill to medium-high, then clean and lightly oil the grill grates. Cut the lemon in half, drizzle with olive oil, and season with salt and freshly ground pepper. Place the lemon halves cut side down on the grill. Cook until golden char marks develop and the lemon is warmed through. Set aside.

Cut the fennel into ¼-inch (6 mm) slices. Heat the skillet over medium-high heat. Add the remaining 1 tablespoon (15 mL) olive oil, and heat for 1 minute. Cook the fennel for 2 minutes or until golden brown and slightly charred. Flip and cook for 1 more minute, then remove into a large bowl.

Add the warm potatoes to the fennel, and toss with the thyme. Squeeze the juice of the charred lemons over the vegetables. Season with salt and freshly ground pepper and drizzle with good-quality olive oil.

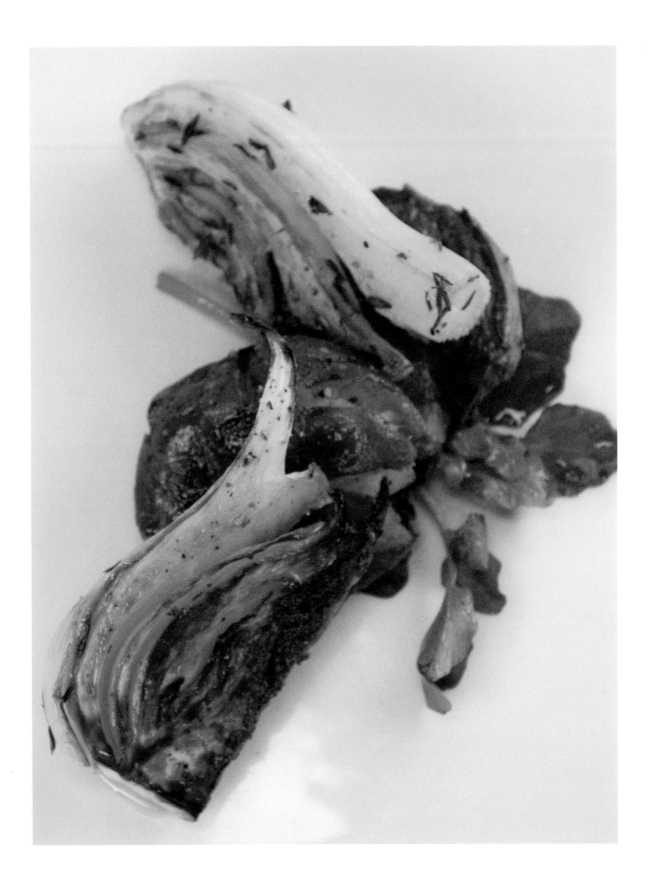

ENSALADA DE QUINOA

Serves 4 to 6

Argentinians have enjoyed the taste and health benefits of quinoa long before it became a popular superfood. Try and find a mix of blond and black varieties.

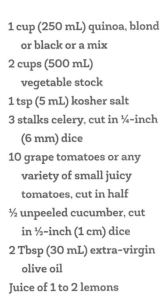

1 cup (250 mL) quinoa, blond or black or a mix

2 cups (500 mL) vegetable stock

1 tsp (5 mL) kosher salt

3 stalks celery, cut in ¼-inch (6 mm) dice

10 grape tomatoes or any variety of small juicy tomatoes, cut in half

½ unpeeled cucumber, cut in ½-inch (1 cm) dice

2 Tbsp (30 mL) extra-virgin olive oil

Juice of 1 to 2 lemons

Place the quinoa in medium saucepan. Rinse well with water a few times and then drain. Add the stock and salt, and bring to a boil over high heat. Reduce the heat to low and cover with lid. Simmer for 15 minutes or until just cooked.

Remove the pot from the heat, and using the tines of a fork, fluff the grains to separate. Transfer to a large bowl.

Add the chopped vegetables and olive oil, and the lemon juice to taste. Season with salt and freshly ground pepper.

HUMITA

Serves 6 as a side dish

Humita is a simple Argentinian peasant dish featuring sweet summer corn. It's thick and almost cake-like, and has been compared to Mexican tamale. The trick here is to extract as much of the sweet milky liquid as you can from the corn.

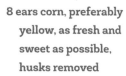

8 ears corn, preferably yellow, as fresh and sweet as possible, husks removed

2 Tbsp (30 mL) unsalted butter

1 Tbsp (15 mL) extra-virgin olive oil

1 cup (250 mL) finely diced onions

½ cup (120 mL) whole milk, divided

1 cup (250 mL) fresh basil leaves

1 tsp (5 mL) red chili flakes, or to taste

Using a box grater, grate the corn kernels into a large bowl. Run the back of a knife down each cob to release the rest of the milky liquid from the kernels into the bowl.

Melt the butter with the olive oil in a Dutch oven or enamelled cast iron pot over medium-low heat. Add the onions and sauté, stirring, until translucent and softened but not browned, about 4 minutes.

Add the corn with all its liquid, and cook, stirring until the mixture thickens, about 10 minutes. Stir in ¼ cup (60 mL) of the milk. Once the milk is absorbed, gradually stir in the remaining ¼ cup (60 mL) milk in 2 additions to ensure even absorption.

Adjust the heat so it stays at a simmer. Cook, stirring, until the corn is creamy, about 4 minutes, depending on the size and freshness of the corn.

Chop the basil and add it to the corn, along with the chili flakes, and salt to taste.

BRAISED LAMB SHANKS WITH CILANTRO-MINT CHIMICHURRI

Serves 6

Malbec is *the* Argentinian red, and the good news is that there are many reasonably priced Malbecs out there. Deep and dark with big tannins (snooty sommeliers call it an "inky" wine), it's a perfect match for the four-hour, low-heat braise of these lamb shanks. Remember—a braising liquid is only as good as the wine you put into it. And check out our super *cool* way to separate the fat from the braising liquid in this recipe.

6 lamb shanks, bone-in

1½ Tbsp (22.5 mL)
    extra-virgin olive oil

2 Tbsp (30 mL) brown sugar

2 medium Spanish onions,
    cut in medium dice

3 medium carrots, peeled
    and cut in medium dice

4 stalks celery, cut in
    medium dice

4 cloves garlic, peeled

2 Tbsp (30 mL) tomato paste

3 cups (750 mL) red wine,
    preferably Malbec

2 cups (500 mL) lamb
    or beef stock

1 small bunch fresh thyme

2 sprigs fresh rosemary

2 cinnamon sticks, broken

1 tsp (5 mL) coriander seeds

1½ tsp (7.5 mL) black
    peppercorns

1 bay leaf

4 cups (1 L) ice

Cilantro-mint chimichurri
    (page 40), to serve

Preheat the oven to 325°F (160°C). Season the lamb shanks with salt and freshly ground pepper.

Place an ovenproof skillet large enough to fit the lamb over medium heat, and add the olive oil. Add the brown sugar and stir to dissolve. Add the lamb shanks and sear until golden brown, turning to ensure all sides are caramelized, about 8 minutes. Transfer the shanks to a plate and set aside.

Add the onions, carrots, celery, and garlic to the pan that you used for the lamb, and cook over medium heat until golden brown and slightly soft, stirring constantly to prevent burning. Add the tomato paste.

Deglaze the pan with the wine. Using a wooden spoon, scrape up the brown bits stuck to the bottom of the pan. Add the stock, thyme, rosemary, cinnamon, coriander, peppercorns, and the bay leaf, and a pinch of salt.

Return the shanks to the pan, and any juice that's collected at the bottom of the plate. The liquid in the pan should go three-quarters up the sides of the shanks. Add water or more stock, if necessary.

Cover and braise in the oven for 3½ hours or until fork tender. Remove the cover and cook a further 30 minutes.

Remove from the oven and let the lamb rest in the braising liquid for 20 minutes. Then remove the lamb from the pot, setting it aside covered in foil.

Have ready a large bowl, a large fine-mesh sieve, and a large saucepan that will fit the lamb shanks. Strain the braising liquid into the large bowl; discard the vegetables and aromatics but do not wash the sieve. To remove the excess fat from the sauce, add

...CONTINUED

the ice to the strained liquid. Working quickly, stir the ice and strain the liquid into the saucepan.

Set the saucepan over medium-low heat, and reduce the liquid by half or until your desired consistency for sauce. Place the lamb shanks back in the sauce to reheat.

Serve with the cilantro-mint chimichurri.

CILANTRO-MINT CHIMICHURRI
Makes about 1½ (325 mL) cups

This is our version of the famous Argentinian condiment. (See page 47 for a more classic version.) Argentinians put it on everything! It's like summertime in a bowl, is great with anything grilled or fried, and is a nice change from regular salsa. Try using your own blend of herbs too. Chimichurri is best served the same day it's made.

1 cup (250 mL) packed fresh cilantro leaves
½ cup (125 mL) fresh flat-leaf parsley
2 Tbsp (30 mL) fresh mint leaves
1 to 2 serrano chilies, seeds removed, finely chopped
¼ cup (60 mL) fresh lime juice
1 Tbsp (15 mL) honey
½ tsp (2.5 mL) kosher salt
2 Tbsp (30 mL) extra-virgin olive oil

In a food processor, add the cilantro, parsley, mint, chilies, lime juice, honey, and salt, and process until it starts to form a paste. With the food processor running, gradually add the olive oil, continuing to process until the sauce is smooth. Scrape down the sides of the food processor as necessary.

Taste and adjust the seasonings. Transfer the chimichurri to a covered container. Refrigerate for up to 3 hours to meld the flavours.

Bring to room temperature before serving.

GRILLED LAMB CHOPS WITH CILANTRO-MINT CHIMICHURRI

Serves 6

There's something magical about the way onion and rosemary work with lamb—and you'll love the way this marinade keeps the chops juicy when they hit the grill. Grate the onion instead of dicing it—this releases onion water, which is the base of the marinade. Chimichurri is the classic Argentinian sauce—they put it on everything.

1 Spanish onion

3 cloves garlic,
    finely chopped

2 Tbsp (30 mL) freshly
    chopped rosemary

2 Tbsp (30 mL) extra-virgin
    olive oil

12 lamb loin chops or
    12 double chops cut from
    a Frenched rack of lamb,
    2 inches (5 cm) thick,
    trimmed of excess fat

Cilantro-mint chimichurri
    (page 40), to serve

Grate the onion using a box grater into a bowl. Add the garlic, olive oil, and rosemary, and some black pepper and combine. Place the lamb chops in a covered nonreactive container, and pour the marinade over the chops. Toss evenly to coat. Leave in the refrigerator to marinate for 4 hours.

Remove the lamb from the marinade and brush off the excess. Discard the marinade. Drizzle with olive oil and season with salt and freshly ground pepper, and allow the lamb to come to room temperature before grilling.

Preheat the grill to medium-high, then clean and oil the grill grates to prevent sticking.

Grill the lamb. If you're using Frenched lamb chops, slide a piece of aluminum foil under the bones to prevent burning. Cook until deep golden char marks develop, about 4 minutes, then turn the lamb 45 degrees and cook another 2 minutes to get a nice cross-hatch pattern. Make sure the foil remains under the bones. Flip and repeat on the other side (carefully moving the foil again under the bones).

Remove the lamb from the grill, and cover loosely with foil, allowing to rest for 5 minutes. Slather with the chimichurri sauce before serving.

GRILLED TRI-TIP WITH CLASSIC CHIMICHURRI
Serves 4 to 6

Grilled steak is as simple as it gets. The secret here is to marinate the meat in the fabled chimichurri sauce, making the tri-tip tender and flavourful. Tri-tip is cut from the bottom sirloin and has a hearty texture, a cut that's becoming more popular in North America. Ask your butcher for it and she'll be impressed.

1 tri-tip steak, about
  2 lbs (900 g), 1½ inches
  (4 cm) thick
4 cups (1 L) classic
  chimichurri (page 47)

Pour half of the chimichurri over the steak, and allow to marinate overnight.

The next day, allow the steak to come to room temperature. Brush off the marinade and set aside for basting.

Preheat the grill to medium-high, then clean and oil the grill grates.

Wipe off the excess marinade from the steak so that it doesn't burn. Grill the steak for 5 minutes or until nice golden char marks develop. Turn the steak 45 degrees and cook a further 3 minutes. Flip and continue to cook, basting with the reserved chimichurri sauce, until the internal temperature reads 145°F (63°C).

Remove the steak from the grill, and tent loosely with aluminum foil. Let rest for 10 minutes to allow the meat to relax and the juices to redistribute.

Carve the meat, and serve with the remaining chimichurri sauce.

CLASSIC CHIMICHURRI
Makes about 4 cups

Here's a more classic take on the Argentinian condiment.

2 cups (500 mL) finely chopped fresh parsley

¼ cup (60 mL) finely chopped fresh oregano

½ red bell pepper, finely diced

1 small red onion, finely diced

4 cloves garlic, finely chopped

½ tsp (2.5 mL) red chili flakes

¾ cup (185 mL) extra-virgin olive oil

¼ cup (60 mL) red wine vinegar

In a bowl, place the herbs, red pepper, onion, garlic, and chili flakes. Add salt and freshly ground pepper to taste, then add the olive oil and vinegar. Taste and adjust the seasonings.

GRILLED PORK RIBS
Serves 4 to 6

Argentinians know their way around barbecue. These ribs are marinated overnight, slow-baked in the oven, then finished with some high-heat grilling. Perfect served with grilled vegetables like corn, tomatoes, and whole jalapeños.

1 rack baby back pork ribs,
 about 3 lbs (1.4 kg)
Drizzle of extra-virgin olive
 oil, for grilling the ribs

MARINADE
4 green onions, thinly sliced
3 to 4 cloves garlic,
 finely chopped
1 canned chipotle,
 or more to taste
½ cup (125 mL) orange juice
¼ cup (60 mL) vegetable oil
2 Tbsp (30 mL) brown sugar
2 Tbsp (30 mL) molasses
2 Tbsp (30 mL) red
 wine vinegar
2 tsp fresh thyme
2 tsp (10 mL) dried oregano
 (or 2 Tbsp/30 mL freshly
 chopped oregano leaves)
2 tsp (10 mL) smoked paprika
2 tsp (10 mL) red
 chili powder
1 tsp (5 mL) ground cumin
1 Tbsp (15 mL) kosher salt
Pinch of black pepper

Remove the silverskin (the transparent membrane) from the bony side of the rack by sliding a dull knife under the membrane to loosen it at one end, grabbing the end and then peeling it off. Use a paper towel if it's slippery. Rinse the ribs and pat dry. Rub all over with salt and freshly ground pepper.

Place all of the marinade ingredients into a blender or food processor and process until smooth. Taste it and adjust the ingredients and seasonings as desired. Reserve ½ cup (125 mL) for basting.

Place the ribs in a shallow dish and cover with the marinade, rubbing it into both sides of the ribs with your hands. Cover with plastic wrap and refrigerate for at least 3 hours or ideally overnight.

Preheat the oven to 250°F (120°C).

Place the ribs and the marinade on a large piece of aluminum foil. Wrap tightly with more foil, making sure the foil is well sealed around the ribs. Place the foil packet on a baking sheet, and roast in the oven for 3 hours or until tender. Remove the ribs from the oven and let cool.

Preheat the grill, one side to medium-high and the other to medium-low. Clean and oil the grill grates. Drizzle the ribs with olive oil to prevent sticking. Place the ribs onto the hotter part of the grill, and allow to smoke and char on one side for 4 minutes. Once a nice crust has formed, carefully flip and repeat for the other side. Move the ribs to the cooler part of the grill and cook for 5 minutes on each side, brushing them with the reserved marinade.

Remove the ribs from the grill when nicely charred and crispy. Cover loosely with foil, and let rest for 5 minutes before serving.

CHAPA PORK TENDERLOIN WITH ORANGE CONFIT AND POMEGRANATE SALSA

Serves 4 to 6, and makes a 1-quart (1 L) jar of orange confit

Chapa is an Argentinian technique of cooking food on a big cast iron surface over open wood fires. But all you need is a good cast iron skillet that's nice and hot (really hot!) so that the meat chars. When the salt- and sugar-crusted pork hits the dry pan, the orange confit sears into the flesh. Using the confit technique on orange peels mellows them out. Use the extra in desserts and cocktails, and even thinly sliced in salads.

ORANGE CONFIT

3 oranges, washed well

1 cup (250 mL) extra-virgin olive oil, or more to cover

1 bay leaf

1 tsp (5 mL) black peppercorns

½ cup (125 mL) white wine, preferably Riesling

½ cup (125 mL) water

CHAPA PORK TENDERLOIN

2 pork tenderloins, about 1 lb (450 g) each, silverskin removed

2 Tbsp (30 mL) fresh thyme leaves

1½ tsp (7.5 mL) kosher salt, or to taste

3 Tbsp (45 mL) light brown sugar

6 pieces orange confit, about 2 inches (5 cm) long

4 Tbsp (60 mL) oil from the confit, divided

Fleur de sel, to finish

Pomegranate salsa (page 52)

ORANGE CONFIT: Slice 2-inch-wide (5 cm) pieces of peel from the orange from top to bottom. Using a sharp knife, remove as much of the white pith from the orange peel. Juice the oranges.

Place the orange peel into a medium saucepan, and add the olive oil, bay leaf, peppercorns, white wine, water, and orange juice. Place the pan over medium-high heat, bring to a boil, then reduce the heat to low and simmer for 25 minutes. Allow to cool in the hot liquid.

Store in a 1-quart (1 L) jar. Keeps for several weeks in the refrigerator.

PORK TENDERLOIN: Place the tenderloins on individual pieces of plastic wrap large enough to wrap the tenderloin. Sprinkle with the thyme and the salt, then the brown sugar, and pat it down firmly with your hand.

Tear or cut the orange confit into ½-inch (1 cm) pieces, and scatter over the meat. Drizzle with the oil from the confit. Tightly wrap the tenderloin with the plastic wrap so that the ingredients will "bond" with the meat. Refrigerate for 1 hour.

Have your oven fat set to the highest setting. You'll be cooking with hot sugar, so take extra caution. Do not get any of the burnt sugar on your hands.

Remove the pork from the fridge and carefully unwrap. Heat a large cast iron skillet over medium heat until a drop of water sizzles on the surface. Add about a tablespoon (15 mL) of confit oil to pan. Lift each pork tenderloin and place it onto the hot surface. Cook without moving for 3 minutes. If the sugar begins to smoke, remove the pan from the heat for a few moments until the smoke subsides. Return the pan to a lower heat.

. . . CONTINUED

When the sugar on the tenderloin becomes quite dark, turn over the tenderloins. Sear on all sides, cooking the pork for about 10 minutes in total, or until done to your preference. For a nice juicy tenderloin that's a little pink in the middle, the internal temperature will measure 130°F (54°C). (If you want a more well-done tenderloin, preheat the oven to 350°F/180°C before searing. Finish the pork in the oven until the internal temperature reaches up to 160°F/71°C.)

Transfer the meat to a carving board, and allow to rest, tented loosely with aluminum foil, for 5 minutes. Slice and sprinkle with fleur de sel. Serve with pomegranate salsa.

POMEGRANATE SALSA
Serves 4 to 6

A party in a bowl, beautiful to behold. Serve this with tortilla chips as an appetizer, or alongside other grilled meats. Try different herbs—whatever you've got growing in your garden.

1 pomegranate, seeds separated and skin and
   light-coloured membrane removed (see below)
½ small red onion, finely diced
1 small tomato, seeded and finely diced
1 fresh jalapeño pepper, seeds removed, finely chopped
1½ bunches fresh cilantro, chopped
1 bunch fresh flat-leaf parsley, chopped
1½ sprigs fresh mint, roughly chopped
2 tsp (10 mL) lime zest
3 Tbsp (45 mL) fresh lime juice
2 Tbsp (30 mL) extra-virgin olive oil

In a medium bowl, toss together all of the ingredients. Season with salt and white (or black) pepper to taste. Cover, and chill in the refrigerator for at least 2 hours before serving.

HOW TO SEPARATE POMEGRANATE SEEDS
Have a large bowl of cold water ready. Cut the pomegranate in half, and place it in the water. Using your hands, separate the seeds from the pith and the membrane; the seeds will sink and everything else will float to the surface. You can then remove what's floating and simply drain the seeds using a sieve. (If you look up the video for the pomegranate salsa at gustotv.com/oneworldkitchen, you can see how easy this is!)

SHEPHERD'S PIE
Serves 6

Ah, shepherd's pie—the ultimate peasant dish. This Argentinian version features a red wine reduction, fragrant oregano, woodsy rosemary, and smoky paprika. And the sliced hard-boiled eggs layered on top are a nice touch. Making it in one big skillet guarantees easy cleaning and reheating the next day, but you can build the pies in individual ramekins as well.

2 onions, cut in medium dice

2 carrots, peeled
and finely diced

1 Tbsp (15 mL) extra-virgin
olive oil

2 lbs (900 g) ground beef

2 bay leaves

2 tsp (10 mL) freshly
chopped rosemary

2 tsp (10 mL) freshly
chopped oregano

1½ tsp (7.5 mL) ground cumin

1½ tsp (7.5 mL) sweet
Spanish smoked paprika
(pimentón dulce)

1 tsp (5 mL) red chili flakes

1 cup (250 mL) dry red wine,
preferably Malbec

1 lb (450 g) ripe tomatoes,
thinly sliced

1 cup (250 mL) kalamata
olives, pitted

4 large baking potatoes,
peeled and cut into
2-inch (5 cm) chunks

1 cup (250 mL) whole milk

6 large egg yolks

2 hard-boiled eggs, peeled

In a large cast iron skillet, sauté the onions and carrots in the olive oil over medium-high heat, stirring occasionally, until the vegetables soften and begin to brown, about 5 minutes.

Crumble in the ground beef, breaking up the meat with a fork or wooden spoon, and cook until it loses its pink colour, about 4 minutes. Stir in the bay leaves, rosemary, oregano, cumin, paprika, and chili flakes.

Add the red wine, and let it bubble gently for 5 minutes to evaporate the alcohol. Stir in the tomatoes and olives, and season to taste with salt and freshly ground pepper.

Reduce the heat to low and simmer for 20 minutes, or until the meat is very tender and the liquid is reduced but not totally evaporated. (The filling needs to be moist.) Remove the skillet from the heat.

While the meat simmers, put the potatoes in a medium pot with cold water to cover, add a fair amount of salt, and bring to a boil over high heat. Reduce the heat slightly, and let it vigorously simmer until the potatoes are tender when pierced with a fork, about 15 minutes. Drain the potatoes well in a colander, and do not wash the pot. Pass the potatoes through a food mill or a ricer back into the pot.

Bring the milk to a boil, and beat it into the potatoes with a wooden spoon. Beat in the egg yolks one at a time, continuing to beat until the potatoes are well blended, fluffy, and yellow.

Preheat the oven to 375°F (190°C) with the rack positioned in the lower third of the oven.

Cut the hard-boiled eggs into ⅓-inch-thick (1 cm) slices, and arrange them over the meat mixture. Spoon the mashed potatoes on top, and smooth the surface with a spatula. Use the tines of a fork to form fine decorative ridges over the entire surface of the potatoes.

Bake for 35 minutes, or until the potatoes are nicely browned on top. Allow to cool for 15 minutes before serving.

GRILLED OCTOPUS WITH CHAPA POTATOES AND ARUGULA

Serves 3

If you're only familiar with deep-fried calamari, then prepare for an *octo-splosion* of tastes and textures! There really are few things in the world as delicious as charred octopus drizzled with good olive oil and fresh lemon juice. The potatoes are finished in a hot cast iron pan, which we call "on the *chapa*." The octopus needs to be cleaned of its ink sac, stomach, eyes, and beak, but you can get your fishmonger to do this.

2 onions, peeled and quartered

2 carrots, peeled and halved crosswise

2 stalks celery, trimmed and halved crosswise

12 cloves garlic, smashed and peeled, divided

2 bay leaves

1 fresh small octopus, about 2 lbs (900 g), cleaned and well rinsed

4 medium red potatoes, scrubbed

About ¾ cup (185 mL) extra-virgin olive oil, divided, plus more for drizzling

1 Tbsp (15 mL) red wine vinegar

1 tsp (5 mL) kosher salt

1 tsp (5 mL) sweet paprika, or more to taste

Juice of 1 lemon

Lemon wedges

3 cups arugula (750 mL)

½ shallot, thinly sliced

Bring a large pot of water to a boil over high heat. Add the onions, carrots, celery, half the garlic cloves, the bay leaves, and some salt and freshly ground pepper. When the water is boiling, use tongs to hold the octopus by the head over the pot, and lower the tentacles into the water for just 3 seconds.

After lifting out the octopus, and bring the water back to a boil, and repeat the process 2 more times. Place the octopus in the pot, reduce the heat to low, and simmer until the tentacles easily pull away from the head, about 1¼ hours. Turn off the heat and allow to cool in the cooking liquid.

While the octopus simmers, put the potatoes in a large saucepan and add 2 tablespoons (30 mL) of the olive oil, the red wine vinegar, and enough cold water to cover by about 1 inch (2.5 cm). Add the 1 teaspoon (5 mL) salt. Bring to a boil over high heat, boil for 1 minute, then reduce the heat to a simmer and cook until the potatoes are tender, about 15 minutes.

Drain the potatoes. Gently smash them between paper towels or a tea towel using the palm of your hand against a cutting board, keeping the potatoes intact. Drizzle with 2 tablespoons (30 mL) of the olive oil, tossing to coat. Set aside.

Finely chop the remaining 6 cloves of garlic. When the octopus is cool enough to handle, drain it in a colander. Separate the tentacles, discarding the head. If the skin is tough when you try to scratch it with your finger, peel it off; if it's tender, leave it on. Toss in a bowl with the garlic, paprika, and 3 tablespoons (45 mL) of the olive oil (or enough to coat). Season with salt and freshly ground pepper to taste.

...CONTINUED

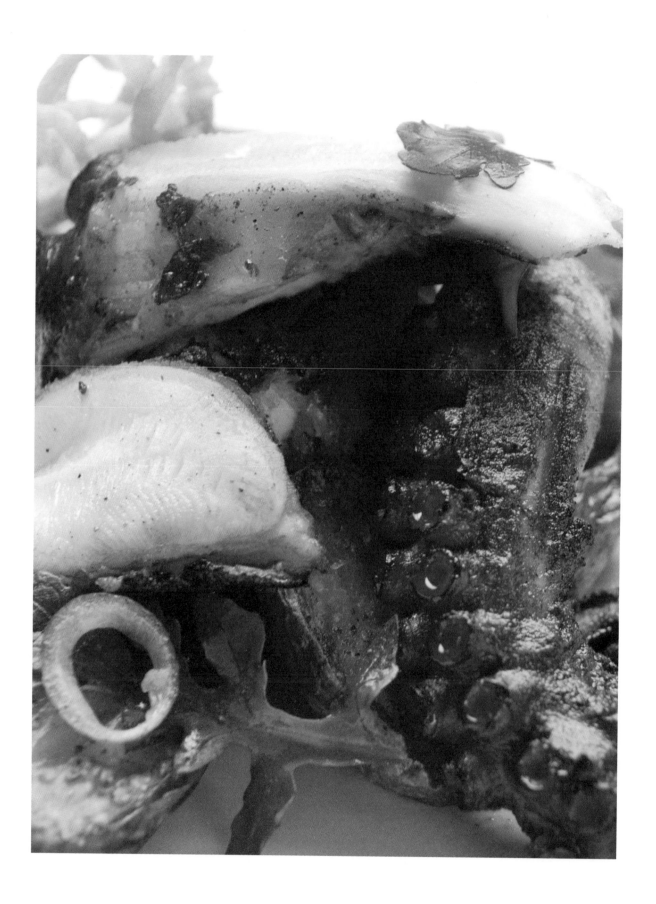

Preheat the grill to medium-high, then clean and oil the grill grates to prevent sticking. Grill the octopus, and cook until rich golden char marks develop. This will take only about 2 minutes per side. (The octopus is already cooked; you're just warming it through as well as adding some flavour and crunch.) Remove from the grill, and cover with aluminum foil to keep warm.

Heat a large cast iron skillet over medium-high heat, and add the remaining ¼ cup (60 mL) olive oil. Place the potatoes on the chapa, and crisp and brown for about 8 minutes without moving. Turn the potatoes. Sear until very crunchy, about 2 minutes on each side, adding more olive oil if necessary.

Cut the octopus into about ½-inch-thick (1 cm) slices, and arrange on a serving plate with the arugula, shallots, and crispy potatoes. Drizzle with olive oil and the juice of the lemon, and season with salt and freshly ground pepper. Serve with the lemon wedges.

SHRIMP WITH SPAETZLE

Serves 6

Argentina has been blessed with successive waves of immigrants from all over the world. Spaetzle is a sort of German pasta and commonly prepared in Argentina. It's a perfect pairing with shrimp.

2 Tbsp (30 mL) kosher
   salt, divided

4 cups (1 L) all-purpose flour

1 tsp (5 mL) freshly ground
   black pepper

4 large eggs, lightly beaten

1 cup (250 mL) water,
   plus more if needed

2 lbs (900 g) large shrimp
   (10/12 count), peeled
   and deveined

1 tsp (5 mL) paprika

3 Tbsp (45 mL) extra-virgin
   olive oil, divided, plus
   more for the spaetzle

4 green onions, white and
   green parts separated,
   finely chopped

2 tsp (10 mL) lemon zest

¼ cup (60 mL) unsalted
   butter (½ stick)

2 cups (500 mL) freshly
   grated Parmesan

½ cup (125 mL) fresh
   flat-leaf parsley

Lemon wedges, to serve

½ cup (125 mL) shaved
   Parmesan to serve,
   or more to taste

Bring a large pot of water to a boil over high heat, and add 1 tablespoon (15 mL) of the salt. Have ready a metal colander and a large bowl for the cooked spaetzle.

Combine the flour, the remaining 1 tablespoon (15 mL) salt, and the pepper in a large bowl. Make a well in the centre of the flour and add the eggs and 1 cup (250 mL) of the water. Using just your fingertips at first, and then gradually spreading your fingers apart, quickly work the flour into the eggs and water to form a thick, lump-free batter, adding more water if necessary.

Season the shrimp with salt and freshly ground pepper, and toss them in a bowl with the paprika and about 1 tablespoon (15 mL) olive oil to coat. Set it aside.

Once your water is boiling vigorously, push about one-quarter of the batter through the metal colander into the water, using a plastic pastry scraper or rubber spatula to force it through the holes. The spaetzle is done when it rises to the surface. Remove it with a large slotted spoon or skimmer as it rises and transfer to a large bowl. Toss the spaetzle with a drizzle of olive oil to prevent it from sticking together. Repeat with the remaining batter.

Heat a large cast iron skillet over medium heat and add the remaining 2 tablespoons (30 mL) olive oil and the spaetzle to the pan. Stir in the white parts of the green onions, the lemon zest, and the butter, and sprinkle the grated Parmesan over the top. Cook until the spaetzle is lightly browned on the bottom. Turn with a spatula and brown on the other side.

Meanwhile, heat another large skillet over medium-high heat. Add the shrimp and sauté for about 2 minutes on each side, until just cooked through and it's crunchy and bright pink.

Place your spaetzle on a serving platter and arrange the shrimp on top. Sprinkle with parsley, the greens part of the green onions, and the shaved Parmesan, and serve with lemon wedges.

PAN-FRIED TROUT WITH BROWN BUTTER

Serves 4

There are many deep clean rivers and lakes in Argentina, meaning there is plenty of trout. Lemon, hazelnuts, and butter are a classic flavour pairing. This recipe can easily be made *à la minute* on a busy weeknight, with a nice salad and some crusty bread on the side—and it helps that trout is still relatively inexpensive. The outside of the trout varies from brown to speckled and the flesh is a gorgeous ochre orange. It's a beautiful-looking dinner.

½ cup (125 mL) unsalted butter (1 stick), for the brown butter

1 to 2 Tbsp (15–30 mL) fresh lemon juice

1 lb (450 g) trout fillets, skin on with the scales removed, whole or separated into 4 portions

1 Tbsp (15 mL) butter, for the trout

1 Tbsp (15 mL) olive or vegetable oil

½ cup (125 mL) finely chopped fresh parsley

½ cup (125 mL) roughly chopped toasted hazelnuts (see below)

Fresh lemon wedges

Begin by making the brown butter. Place the ½ cup (125 mL) butter in a heavy saucepan with a light-coloured bottom so that you can monitor the browning. Over low heat, melt the butter and cook, stirring frequently, until the butter solids collecting at the bottom of the saucepan turn a deep golden brown with a nutty scent. This will take about 6 or 7 minutes.

Remove the pan from the heat, and skim off and discard the foam. Stir in the lemon juice and set aside. Keep warm.

Season the trout with salt and freshly ground pepper. In a large skillet, heat the 1 tablespoon (15 mL) butter and the oil over medium-high heat. Add the trout, skin side down, and fry until the edges begin to turn golden and crisp, about 2 minutes. Turn over the fillets using a metal fish spatula or flipper, and finish cooking, about 2 more minutes, depending on the thickness of the fish and your desired doneness.

To check for doneness, use the tip of a small knife and flake some of the flesh. It should be glossy in the very centre and slightly translucent pink. (Or cook for longer if preferred. Keep in mind that fish will continue to cook even if it's taken off the heat.)

Transfer the trout to serving plates. Drizzle each fillet with a small spoonful of the warm brown butter. Garnish with the parsley and hazelnuts, and serve with the wedges of lemon.

HOW TO TOAST AND PEEL HAZELNUTS
Place the whole nuts on a baking sheet in a 325°F (160°C) oven until lightly browned, aromatic, and the skins begin to split. Empty the nuts onto a slightly damp tea towel. Wrap them up tightly for 5 minutes, and then rub them vigorously while still wrapped in the tea towel. Much of the skin will loosen and can be removed.

SEAFOOD STEW
Serves 4 to 6

This seafood stew (*cazuela de mariscos*) is best served with a huge family-style salad and lots of fresh crusty bread. The onion, garlic, and carrot provide a traditional aromatic base while the red and yellow peppers add colour and sweetness. The broth is perfumed by the clam juice, white wine, and coconut milk, and once the clams and mussels open, the liquor they release infuses the coconut broth with even more of a taste of the sea.

1 Tbsp (15 mL) extra-virgin olive oil

1 Tbsp (15 mL) butter

1 cup (250 mL) finely diced Spanish onion

½ cup (125 mL) diced yellow bell pepper (medium dice)

½ cup (125 mL) diced red bell pepper (medium dice)

1 cup (250 mL) finely diced carrots

2 tsp (10 mL) finely chopped garlic

1½ cups (375 mL) light coconut milk

1 cup (250 mL) bottled or canned clam juice

½ cup (125 mL) white wine, preferably Sauvignon Blanc

1 Tbsp (15 mL) tomato paste

½ tsp (2.5 mL) Spanish paprika

1 cup (250 mL) heavy cream (optional)

2 lbs (900 g) shrimp (21/25 count), peeled and deveined with tails left on

1 lb (450 g) fresh mussels, scrubbed and beards removed

12 littleneck clams, scrubbed

2 baby squid, cut into ¼-inch (6 mm) rings, tentacles left whole

2 Tbsp (30 mL) freshly chopped cilantro, for garnish

2 Tbsp (30 mL) freshly chopped flat-leaf parsley, for garnish

1 loaf crunchy rustic bread, to serve

Lemon wedges, to serve

In a large sauté pan over medium heat, melt the butter in the olive oil. Add the onions, peppers, carrots, and garlic, and sauté until tender and the onions are translucent, about 5 minutes. Stir occasionally being careful not to let the vegetables brown. Season with salt and freshly ground pepper.

Add the coconut milk, clam juice, wine, tomato paste, and paprika, increase the heat to medium-high, and bring to a simmer. Simmer uncovered for 10 minutes. Season with salt and freshly ground pepper. Add the cream, if using.

Add the 4 kinds of seafood and cover the pan. Reduce the heat to medium, and cook until the clams and mussels open and the shrimp are plump, bright pink, and just losing their translucent colour, another 2 minutes.

Remove the pan from the heat, discarding any unopened shells. Ladle into bowls and garnish with the cilantro and parsley. Serve hot with lots of crunchy warm bread and wedges of lemon.

CARAMELIZED ENDIVES WITH VINEGAR

Serves 4 as a side dish

An incredibly simple and unique side dish. Serve it alongside a nice piece of fish or a juicy steak.

½ cup (125 mL) red wine vinegar (or ¼ cup/60 mL if you prefer a sweeter dish)

4 medium endives, trimmed

⅓ cup (80 mL) granulated sugar

Preheat a large cast iron skillet over medium-high heat.

Cut the endives in half lengthwise. Pour the vinegar into a shallow bowl, and dip the endives in the vinegar, turning to coat. Reserve the vinegar.

Sprinkle the sugar evenly over the hot cooking surface. When the sugar begins to melt, place the endive halves cut side down on the hot surface, not letting them move for 3 minutes. Keep a close watch on the sugar so it doesn't burn, lowering the heat if it starts to do so. (Always use caution when working with melted sugar.)

Once the endives are nicely caramelized on one side, turn them over and carefully pour the reserved vinegar around the endives—not over them or you'll dissolve the caramelized sugar. Cook until they are tender and glazed, about 3 more minutes.

Remove from the pan and serve.

CINNAMON CHURROS WITH CHOCOLATE SAUCE

Serves 4, and makes 1½ cups (375 mL) chocolate sauce

Once you've made churros, you'll never go back to doughnuts. Crispy on the outside, churros are delicate, sweet, and light as air inside. They are shaped as little tubes instead of rounds, and you can dust them with cinnamon sugar or icing sugar as soon as they come out of the oil. Then dunk them in chocolate sauce—it's worth every calorie. And *always* make more than you need.

CHOCOLATE SAUCE

1¼ cups (310 mL)
   heavy cream
1 cup (250 mL) finely
   chopped semisweet
   70% chocolate

CINNAMON SUGAR

1 tsp (5 mL) ground
   cinnamon
2 Tbsp (30 mL) granulated
   sugar

CHURROS

1 cup (250 mL) water
2½ Tbsp (37.5 mL)
   granulated sugar
½ tsp (2.5 mL) kosher salt
2 Tbsp (30 mL) vegetable oil
1 cup (250 mL) all-purpose
   flour
Vegetable oil for deep-frying,
   about 4 cups (1 L)
Piping bag with a medium
   star-shaped tip
Kitchen scissors

CHOCOLATE SAUCE: In a medium saucepan over medium heat, add the cream. Let it come to a gentle simmer, making sure it doesn't boil. Place the chocolate in a heatproof bowl, then pour the hot cream over the chocolate and cover the bowl with plastic wrap. Allow to sit for 4 minutes, or until the chocolate is melted. Remove the plastic wrap, and whisk or stir to combine. Set aside.

CINNAMON SUGAR: In a small bowl, mix the sugar and cinnamon just to combine. Set aside.

CHURROS: In a small saucepan over medium heat, combine the water, sugar, salt, and vegetable oil. Bring to a boil, then remove the pan from the heat. Using a wooden spoon, beat in the flour until thick paste forms. Return the pan to the heat, and cook for another minute.

Heat the oil in a heavy-bottomed pot or wok over medium-high heat to 375°F (191°C). Line a baking sheet with paper towels.

Place the dough into the piping bag. Pipe dough about 2½ inches (6 cm) in length into the oil, use scissors to cut the dough. Do 3 or 4 at a time so as not to overcrowd the pot. Deep-fry until golden brown and crispy, about 4 minutes. Remove using a slotted spoon or spider and let drain on the paper towel-lined baking sheet. Immediately toss with the cinnamon sugar to ensure the coating will stick. Repeat with the remaining batter.

Serve warm or at room temperature with the chocolate sauce.

POACHED PEARS IN RED WINE WITH CARDAMOM AND ORANGE

Serves 4

We obviously recommend using a Malbec, the quintessential Argentinian wine. As for your pear selection, go with whatever your market has that's ripe but still firm; our favourite is Anjou. The mascarpone cream is rich, thick, and heavenly, but in a pinch you could substitute a great vanilla ice cream. See the tip on page 63 on how to toast and peel hazelnuts.

1 bottle (750 mL) red wine, preferably Malbec

1 cup (250 mL) granulated sugar

Zest of 1 orange

3 cardamom pods, smashed

1 cinnamon stick

4 pears, peeled, stems left intact

½ cup (125 mL) toasted chopped hazelnuts, to serve

MASCARPONE CREAM

½ cup (125 mL) mascarpone cheese

½ vanilla bean, seeds scraped

¾ cup (185 mL) heavy cream

3 Tbsp (45 mL) icing sugar

In a large heavy-bottomed saucepan, combine the wine, sugar, orange zest, cardamom, and cinnamon over medium heat, stirring until the sugar dissolves and the mixture comes to simmer.

Add the pears and return the mixture to a simmer. If the liquid doesn't cover the pears completely, add some water. Reduce the heat to a simmer, and cook until the pears are tender yet slightly firm when pierced with knife, about 15 minutes, depending on the size of the pear.

Allow the pears to cool in the poaching liquid. Once cool, remove the pears and set aside. Strain the poaching liquid into another saucepan. Reduce the liquid over medium-low heat down to about 1 cup (250 mL). Allow the sauce to cool.

MASCARPONE CREAM: In a bowl, lightly beat the mascarpone with a wooden spoon to soften. Add the scraped vanilla seeds. In a separate bowl, whip the cream with the icing sugar until soft peaks form. Gently fold the whipped cream into the mascarpone in 3 separate additions. Set aside in the refrigerator.

FINISH THE POACHED PEARS: You can serve the pears and the sauce at room temperature or cold from the fridge. To serve, place one pear standing up on a serving plate. (If the pear is tipsy, slice a small amount from the bottom of the pear to create a flat surface.). Drizzle with the sauce, and serve with a dollop of mascarpone cream and a scattering of crunchy hazelnuts.

CRÊPES WITH DULCE DE LECHE
Serves 6 to 8

This might be the best dessert ever in the history of the world. And it's just too much fun to make. Take a can (yes, the *whole* can) of condensed milk and simmer it in water for three hours. Inside, it slowly caramelizes and turns into a thick, sweet nectar that you can then drizzle over your crêpes. Top with whipped cream and nuts. Crazy good.

1 can (14 oz/300 mL) sweetened condensed milk

4 large eggs

¾ cup (185 mL) whole milk

¾ cup (185 mL) half-and-half cream

1 cup (250 mL) all-purpose flour

3 Tbsp (45 mL) melted butter

Vegetable oil, for frying crêpes

2 cups (500 mL) heavy cream, for whipping

2 Tbsp (30 mL) icing sugar

1 tsp (5 mL) vanilla extract

½ cup (125 mL) coarsely chopped toasted almonds or hazelnuts, for garnish (optional)

For the dulce de leche, place the unopened can of condensed milk in a large pot. Cover the can completely with water. Place the pan over medium-high heat and bring the water to a simmer. Reduce the heat to low and cover the pot.

Gently simmer for exactly 3 hours with the lid on, adding water as necessary to keep the can covered. Do not leave unattended. (You should only attempt this recipe if you don't plan to leave the kitchen for the entire 3 hours.) After the 3 hours are up, carefully remove the can using tongs. Allow to cool slightly for 20 minutes.

In a large bowl, beat the eggs and whisk in the milk and cream and a pinch of salt. Add the flour and melted butter. Continue whisking until the mixture becomes like a thin pancake batter. Strain the batter through a fine-mesh sieve, and let rest for 1 hour.

Have ready a baking sheet or large plates to spread out the crêpes as you cook them. Heat an 8-inch (20 cm) skillet or crêpe pan over medium-high heat, and add a little oil into the pan just to coat. Pour ¼ cup (60 mL) of the batter into the pan, and swirl the pan around to make a thin crêpe.

Cook on one side for about 1 minute, and then flip. Cook the other side for 30 seconds. Repeat with the remaining batter, and lay out the crêpes separately on the baking sheet or plates. Let them cool completely before stacking.

To whip the cream, in a large cold stainless-steel bowl, add the cream, sugar, and vanilla. Using a large wire whisk, whisk the cream until light, fluffy, and billowy. Transfer to a nonreactive bowl or container, and keep covered in the refrigerator.

To assemble, place one crêpe on a cutting board. Using a small offset spatula or butter knife, evenly smear 2 tablespoons (30 mL) of the room-temperature dulce de leche on the crêpe, leaving a 1-inch (2.5 cm) border. Top with another crêpe and repeat. Roll up like a cigar. Continue with the remaining crêpes. Slice into 1½-inch (4 cm) pieces. (If it's hard to slice, trying chill it in the refrigerator for 30 minutes before again, but let the slices come to room temperature before serving.)

ITALY

Vanessa Gianfrancesco

All my life, food has been a source of inspiration. My earliest memories are set behind countertops and tables, where I was surrounded by ingredients whose names I didn't always know but whose flavours I was already able to recognize. My grandmothers and mother took me under their wing in the hopes that I would carry on their recipes and traditions. More than twenty years later, I would like to think I have accomplished just that.

My family says that I was born cooking! By eighteen months, I was already beside my mother rolling out pasta dough into long logs. I wasn't quite able to shape the pasta perfectly, but I simply loved helping, so my family could never say no to me. In fact, at every chance I got I would have an adult pull a chair up to the counter so I could participate in stirring something. That would probably explain why, on my second birthday, I received my very own little apron, oven mitts, and a rolling pin!

Some of my other best recollections are of spending summer vacations in my grandmother's kitchen where I'd help her prepare meals for our family of fourteen. Every morning I'd go to my grandmother's house, and over breakfast we'd discuss what to make for dinner, usually based on what was growing in the garden. Sometimes we'd walk to the grocery store where I could occasionally convince her what to buy. While the rest of the kids played outside, I'd learn and experiment with recipes—from fresh pastas to minestrones made with vegetables from our garden. My six cousins and I would then turn her house into a restaurant, setting up tables and bringing out the wineglasses, all while the food bubbled away in the kitchen.

My hungry Italian family was the perfect test group. By age twelve, I proudly cooked a meal of my very own, a simple dish of different meats and root vegetables slow-roasted in our fireplace for six hours. How I got the idea, and how I thought of executing it, still astounds my family to this day. Cooking for my family is probably where my deeply rooted passion for cooking and entertaining comes from.

The smell of freshly baked bread or pizza is something I will never forget. But Italian cuisine is about so much more than pizza and pasta—it's about how seriously food is taken in Italian culture. We love food, we appreciate food, and we love sharing meals with friends and family. We linger over a meal; it's almost unheard of to eat standing up or finish a meal in less than an hour.

After travelling and eating my way through Italy, I came to know the diversity of its culinary regions. In the north of Italy, it's about the cheeses, beans, cured meats, and dishes like risotto or polenta. And in the south of Italy, it's all about fresh fish, olive oils, and pastas. Cooking in Italy is about maximizing local produce, making sure to use what's freshly available and in season. I met a lot of Italians priding themselves on the fresh ingredients you could get locally, ingredients that made the simplest of dishes breathtakingly good.

Despite food being my lifelong obsession, it wasn't exactly what I had planned careerwise. I finished my bachelor's degree, job-shadowed for a lawyer, and could in no way see myself doing this for the rest of my life! I was cooking and catering professionally on the side and gaining some hands-on experience in the business. So it was time to pursue professional training, and I enrolled in the Institut de tourisme et d'hôtellerie du Québec, the culinary institute in Montreal. I worked under some remarkable chefs and learned technique, discipline, and a new respect for food—even a newer respect for the food of my heritage.

"What type of chef are you?" is a question I hear often. Well, I'm a chef who takes classic Italian recipes and adapts them to the modern-day palate. That is, I'm following the ethos of Italian cuisine. As you go through this chapter, you'll probably be familiar with most of the recipe names. That's because Italian cuisine is about not inventing recipes but rather modernizing the classics and making them your own. Remember, you never have to follow a recipe down to the letter. If you're making my risotto, for example, but don't have all the ingredients, swap out a couple of them and make it your own. And it's not about expensive ingredients either. Cooking is about the experience, from the time you decide what to make to finding the ingredients, putting the stove on, and enjoying the final meal with the ones you love or when you just want to spoil yourself.

I've included my all-time favourites in this chapter. It almost feels like passing down family secrets! Sharing recipes is a very humbling experience; I feel privileged and honoured that people are willing to learn about the food I love preparing. I hope these recipes will someday become your family favourites too. There might be a good chance of that happening—after all, my recipes are intended to be simple and easy . . . just the way I like it.

Recipes

ROSEMARY AND OLIVE FOCACCIA

Makes one 8-inch (20 cm) square focaccia

Perhaps focaccia is to Italy what baguette is to France. Chewy, crusty focaccia is great for sandwiches or served on its own dipped in some good-quality EVOO and balsamic. Here we've added rosemary and olives on top, but you can add anything you like. Dried figs, caramelized onions, and thyme is another great combination.

1 tsp (5 mL) active dry yeast

1 cup (250 mL) warm water (about 110°F/43°C), divided

2 tsp (10 mL) granulated sugar or honey

¼ cup (60 mL) extra-virgin olive oil, for the dough

About 2⅔ cups (660 mL) (11 oz/310 g) bread flour, plus more for dusting the work surface

1½ tsp (7.5 mL) kosher salt

½ cup (125 mL) roughly chopped kalamata olives (pitted)

2 tsp (10 mL) roughly chopped fresh rosemary

About 3 Tbsp (45 mL) extra-virgin olive oil for brushing the dough and pan and for drizzling

In a small bowl, combine the yeast and ¼ cup (60 mL) of the warm water. Let it sit for 10 minutes, or until the mixture starts to foam and gives off a yeasty aroma. Add the ¼ cup (60 mL) olive oil, sugar (or honey), and the remaining ¾ cup (190 mL) water; stir to combine and dissolve the sugar.

In a large bowl, stir together the flour and salt. Pour in the yeast mixture into the flour, mixing to incorporate. Transfer the mixture to a lightly floured work surface. Knead the dough, adding a bit of flour to the work surface as necessary, until it is smooth, soft, and not tacky, about 10 minutes. Place the dough in a lightly oiled bowl, and cover with plastic wrap. Let rise in a warm place until doubled in size, about 1 hour or more depending on the temperature of the room.

Grease an 8-inch (20 cm) square pan with 1 teaspoon (5 mL) of olive oil. Place the dough in the pan and begin pressing it out to fit the size of the pan. Turn the dough over, and drizzle with another 1 teaspoon (5 mL) of olive oil. Continue to stretch the dough to fit the pan. As you are doing so, spread your fingers out to make holes in the dough about 1 to 2 inches (2.5–5 cm) apart. Top with the olives and rosemary. Cover the pan with plastic wrap, and let rest it in a warm place until doubled in size.

Preheat the oven to 425°F (220°C).

Remove the plastic wrap, brush the dough with 2 tablespoons (30 mL) olive oil, and sprinkle with 1 teaspoon (5 mL) or so of coarse sea salt or your favourite crunchy finishing salt. Bake until the top of the loaf is golden brown, about 20 minutes. Let it cool slightly before slicing and serving.

Serve with your favourite olive oil and balsamic vinegar.

TARALLI

Makes 2 dozen taralli

Think of these as crunchy little pretzel bites or mini Italian bagels. Dunk these taralli into red wine—Italian, of course—as you relax on the patio with friends. You can also shape these into little bows. They keep for weeks, so think about making an extra batch.

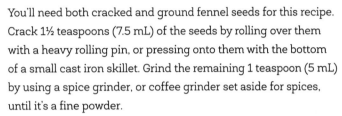

2½ tsp (12.5 mL) fennel
    seeds, divided

2½ tsp (12.5 mL)
    active dry yeast

1 cup (250 mL) dry white
    wine, preferably
    Sauvignon Blanc

¼ cup (60 mL) extra-virgin
    olive oil

1 tsp (5 mL) kosher salt

About 2 cups (500 mL)
    all-purpose flour,
    plus more as needed

1 large egg, for the egg wash

Crunchy finishing salt

You'll need both cracked and ground fennel seeds for this recipe. Crack 1½ teaspoons (7.5 mL) of the seeds by rolling over them with a heavy rolling pin, or pressing onto them with the bottom of a small cast iron skillet. Grind the remaining 1 teaspoon (5 mL) by using a spice grinder, or coffee grinder set aside for spices, until it's a fine powder.

In a medium saucepan, warm the wine to just over room temperature, about 110°F (43°C). Place the yeast in a large bowl and pour over the wine. Let stand until foaming a little, about 10 minutes. Stir in the olive oil, salt, and the cracked and ground fennel seed.

Add as much of the flour as necessary until you have a slightly sticky, shaggy dough. Turn out onto a clean work surface. (You shouldn't have to add flour to the work surface because of the olive oil in the dough, but of course do so if it is sticking.) Knead until slightly smooth, adding flour if necessary, about 5 minutes. Let it rest on the work surface covered with a damp tea towel for 10 minutes. Then knead again until the dough is smooth and elastic, about 7 minutes. (All this kneading is developing the right amount of gluten for taralli.)

Place the dough in a lightly oiled bowl, then turn over the dough to coat it lightly with oil. Cover the bowl with plastic wrap, and let rise in a warm place until the dough is puffy but not quite doubled, about 30 minutes, depending on the dough and the temperature.

Break off a piece of dough the size of a walnut, and roll it between your palms and fingers to form a rope about as thin as a pencil. Continue with the rest of the dough, covering the ropes with tea towel as you form them.

. . . CONTINUED

Have ready a lightly greased baking sheet. Cut each rope into 4-inch-long (10 cm) pieces, and shape them into rings about 2 inches (5 cm) in diameter. Press the ends together very firmly to keep them from separating during baking. Set the rings on the baking sheet, cover them with a clean tea towel, and let rise slightly, about 1 hour.

When the hour is almost up, preheat the oven to 350°F (180°C). Line 2 baking sheets with parchment paper, and a third with paper towels.

Fill a wide braising pan or large pot halfway with water and bring to a boil. Plunge about 7 taralli into the boiling water. They will either sink or float. If they sink, wait for them to rise to the surface, then flip them over and cook for 1 minute; if they float, cook them for 1 minute on each side.

Remove the taralli with a slotted spoon or spider, and drain on the paper towels, letting them cool slightly. Transfer to the parchment-lined baking sheets.

For the egg wash, in a small bowl whisk the egg with 2 teaspoons (10 mL) water. Using a pastry brush, brush the taralli lightly with the egg wash, then sprinkle with the salt.

Bake until crispy and golden brown, about 7 minutes. Allow to cool and serve.

DEEP-FRIED STUFFED OLIVES

Serves 6 or more

Go figure: the Italians have found yet another thing to do with olives—stuffed, no less, then breaded and deep-fried. Who knew you could pack so much flavour into one little olive? Try serving a big platter of these the next time you have guests over, and see how long they last.

2 tsp (10 mL) extra-virgin olive oil

6 oz (170 g) ground veal or ground lean pork

1 tsp (5 mL) freshly chopped rosemary

1 tsp (5 mL) freshly chopped sage

1 tsp (5 mL) freshly chopped thyme

¾ cup (185 mL) white wine, preferably Verdicchio or another sharp, bright Italian wine

4 oz (110 g) prosciutto, finely chopped (about ¾ cup/185 mL)

3 oz (85 g) Parmesan, grated (about ¾ cup/185 mL)

3 oz (85 g) pecorino Romano cheese, grated (about ¾ cup/185 mL)

1 cup (250 mL) Italian breadcrumbs, divided, more if necessary

Pinch of freshly grated nutmeg

1 tsp (5 mL) crumbled dried red chili

1 tsp (5 mL) lemon zest

3 large eggs, divided

2 lbs (900 g) green olives (about 2 cups/500 mL), cracked and pitted

¾ cup (185 mL) all-purpose flour

Vegetable oil for deep-frying, about 4 cups (1 L)

In a large skillet over on medium-high, heat the olive oil. Add the veal (or pork), and season with salt and freshly ground pepper. Cook for 5 minutes, or until lightly browned. Add the 3 herbs, and mix to combine. Add the white wine and stir, allowing the wine to evaporate. Transfer the meat to a large bowl and allow to cool.

Add the prosciutto, the Parmesan and the pecorino, half of the breadcrumbs, the nutmeg, chili, and lemon zest, and one egg. Mix to combine. If the mixture is too wet, add more breadcrumbs. Carefully stuff the olives with this mixture using your hands.

Make a breading station by placing the flour in one bowl, the rest of the breadcrumbs in a second bowl, and the remaining 2 eggs in the third. Whisk the eggs.

Have ready a baking sheet for the breaded olives, and line a large plate or baking sheet with paper towels. With one hand, dunk a few olives at a time in the flour to lightly coat; this will help the egg to stick to the slippery olive. Then dunk into the eggs and roll around just to coat. Finally place into the breadcrumb mixture and toss gently to coat. Shake off any excess and place on the baking sheet.

In a deep, heavy-bottomed pan or wok over medium-high heat, heat the oil to 375°F (191°C). Deep-fry the olives in small batches, about 8 at a time, until golden brown and crunchy. Use a slotted spoon or spider to remove the olives from the oil, and let drain on the paper towels. Repeat with remaining olives.

Enjoy with lots of chilled Verdicchio.

BAGNA CAUDA
Serves 6 as an appetizer

This is a stunning starter dish to share with friends and family over drinks or before dinner. An assortment of fresh veggies dipped in a warm olive oil and butter bath perfumed with garlic and anchovies? Perfect. And don't skimp on the anchovies!

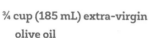

¾ cup (185 mL) extra-virgin
  olive oil
6 Tbsp (90 mL) unsalted
  butter (¾ stick), room
  temperature
12 anchovy fillets
  (salt- or oil-packed),
  roughly chopped
6 large cloves garlic, chopped
Assorted fresh vegetables
  (such as mushrooms,
  carrots, snow peas,
  peppers, and cherry
  tomatoes), cut into
  bite-size pieces
1 loaf crusty Italian or
  French bread, cut into
  2-inch (5 cm) pieces
Fondue pot, or a flameproof
  dish with a small tabletop
  alcohol or gas burner

In a food processor or blender, process the olive oil, butter, anchovies, and garlic until smooth. Transfer to a heavy-bottomed medium saucepan.

Cook over low heat for 15 minutes, stirring occasionally. The sauce will separate. Season with salt and freshly ground pepper.

Pour the sauce into a fondue pot (or a flameproof dish set over a small alcohol or gas burner) so that you can serve it warm. Serve with the vegetables and bread.

PROSCIUTTO-WRAPPED SAMBUCA SHRIMP

Serves 5 as an appetizer (2 shrimp per person)

Consider this: salty ham wrapped around sweet shrimp meat, then pan-fried till crispy and finished in a flambée *whoosh*! As the alcohol burns off the sambuca, it leaves a rich, licorice-flavoured drizzle. *Yum*. Remember, the trick to flambéeing is to tilt the pan away from you after you've poured in the sambuca. This moves the flammable fumes closer to the heat source (and farther from you). Once the flambée starts, just set the skillet down and let it burn out naturally. Stopping the burn with a lid traps in the unwanted alcohol and leaves an acrid taste in the dish.

10 slices prosciutto

5 to 8 fresh sage leaves, roughly chopped

10 large shrimp (14/16 count), peeled and deveined with tails left on

2 Tbsp (30 mL) extra-virgin olive oil

2 Tbsp (30 mL) sambuca

1 Tbsp (15 mL) butter (optional)

Lay a piece of prosciutto on the work surface, and sprinkle with the sage. Wrap the shrimp with the prosciutto, leaving the tail end showing. Repeat with remaining shrimp.

Have ready a small heatproof container for the excess oil. Heat a large nonstick skillet over medium heat, and add the olive oil. Cook the shrimp until the prosciutto is golden brown, about 3 minutes. Flip and repeat until the shrimp is cooked and the prosciutto is golden brown and crispy.

Remove the pan from the heat. Drain the excess oil from the pan by carefully tilting the pan to one side and pouring the oil into the small container. Discard the oil.

If you're using an electric stove, have a match ready. Return the pan to the stove over medium-high heat, and add the sambuca. If you're using a gas stove, carefully tilt the pan away from you to ignite the gases and to make sure the flames are far from your hand. If using an electric stove, use a match, holding it right above the shrimp at the edge of the pan. Once it starts flaming, just let it burn out naturally without covering the pan.

Scrape up the brown bits at the bottom of the pan, and add the butter, if using. Serve immediately.

GRILLED CAESAR SALAD
Serves 4

Our take on the classic Caesar salad will spoil you for all others. The secret? Brushing the romaine leaves with pancetta fat and then grilling them for a few seconds. It gives the salad a warm, smoky flavour. And, yes, you're reading the recipe correctly: we call for ten anchovy fillets in the dressing. Fear not.

8 slices pancetta
  (⅛-inch/3 mm slices)
1 head romaine
8 slices baguette
1 clove garlic, peeled
1 Tbsp (15 mL) extra-virgin
  olive oil
Extra-virgin olive oil
  for drizzling
¾ cup (185 mL) shaved
  Parmesan
1 lemon, cut into wedges

CAESAR DRESSING
2 large egg yolks
2 cloves garlic, peeled
10 anchovy fillets
  (salt- or oil-packed)
Juice of 2 lemons,
  plus more to taste
1 cup (250 mL) extra-virgin
  olive oil
Splash of water
Freshly cracked pepper

Preheat the oven to 325°F (160°C).

Line a large plate with paper towels. Place the pancetta on a parchment paper–lined baking sheet, and cook for 5 to 6 minutes or until slightly crisp and golden but still slightly soft. Drain on the paper towels and set aside. Pour the pan drippings into a small saucepan and set aside.

CAESAR DRESSING: Place the egg yolk, garlic, anchovies, and lemon juice and some black pepper into a mini food processor, and process until smooth. Slowly add the olive oil in a steady stream through the feed tube. The dressing should be well emulsified and taste tangy and creamy. Add more lemon if not tangy enough, or water or more olive oil if too acidic.

PREPARE THE SALAD: Remove any wilted or damaged leaves from the romaine, and cut the romaine into 4 wedges lengthwise. Plunge into a big bowl of cold water to clean, gently swishing them around but making sure they stay intact. Shake off the water and place on a baking sheet.

Heat the saucepan of pancetta drippings over low heat. Brush the cut sides of the romaine with the pancetta drippings, and season with salt and freshly ground pepper to taste.

Preheat the grill to high, then clean and oil the grill grates.

Have ready a plate and the clove of garlic for the crostini. Grill the bread slices until lightly toasted to a golden brown on both sides. Remove from the grill and immediately rub both sides of the bread with the garlic clove. Drizzle with the olive oil. Set aside.

Grill the romaine on a cut side down for just 30 seconds, just to get some deep char marks. Turn the romaine and grill on another side just to finish heating it through, about 10 seconds.

Place a wedge of grilled romaine on each serving plate, and drizzle with some dressing. Top each wedge with Parmesan, 2 pancetta slices, 1 lemon wedge, and 2 crostini.

Serve immediately.

TUSCAN BEAN SOUP

Makes 8 healthy portions

This classic Tuscan soup is rich and thick, and it cries out for crusty bread and a big, fat red wine (Italian, of course!). The secret to a rich, flavourful Italian soup is tossing in a Parmesan rind, which infuses the broth with its sweet, salty goodness. So, hang onto those cheese rinds to flavour your soups, sauces, and stews. For those of you in a hurry, substitute canned beans and remove the overnight soaking process.

1 lb (450 g) dried white beans (about 2¼ cups/560 mL), such as great northern, cannellini, or navy

8 slices pancetta (⅛-inch/3 mm slices)

2 Spanish onions, cut in medium dice

2 Tbsp (30 mL) extra-virgin olive oil

4 cloves garlic, finely chopped

5 cups (1.25 L) chicken stock

1 piece Parmesan rind, 3 by 2 inches (8 × 5 cm)

2 tsp (10 mL) kosher salt

½ tsp (2.5 mL) black pepper

1 bay leaf

2 tsp (10 mL) finely chopped fresh rosemary

6 carrots, halved lengthwise and cut crosswise into ½-inch (1 cm) pieces

11 oz (310 g) cured Italian sausage (preferably soppressata), cut into ½- by ¼-inch (1 cm × 6 mm) pieces

1 lb (450 g) kale, stems and centre ribs removed and discarded, leaves coarsely chopped

1 cup (250 mL) freshly grated or shaved Parmesan, for garnish

2 Tbsp (30 mL) extra-virgin olive oil

Place the dried beans in a bowl and rinse a few times. Cover with plenty of cold water, and soak overnight.

Preheat the oven to 325°F (160°C).

Line a large plate with paper towels. Place the pancetta on a parchment paper–lined baking sheet, and cook until golden brown and crispy, about 5 minutes. Drain and let cool on the paper towels.

Rinse and drain the beans in a colander and set aside. In an 8-quart (8 L) pot, cook the onions in the olive oil over medium-low heat, stirring occasionally, until softened, about 5 minutes. Add the garlic and cook, stirring, for 1 minute.

Add the beans to the pot. Add 2 cups (500 mL) of water and the chicken stock, Parmesan cheese rind, salt, pepper, bay leaf, and rosemary. Bring to a boil over medium-high heat, and then reduce to a simmer and let cook, uncovered, until the beans are just tender, about 40 minutes.

Stir in the carrots, and simmer for 10 minutes or until almost tender but still slightly firm. Add the chopped sausage, kale, and 4–5 cups water. Simmer uncovered, stirring occasionally, until the kale is tender, about 4 minutes.

Taste the soup and adjust the seasonings with salt and freshly ground pepper. Ladle into serving bowls, and top with the pancetta rounds and Parmesan.

GNOCCHI
Serves 6

Every once in a while, Italians get tired of pasta, and that's why they invented gnocchi. Also, *gnocchi* is kind of a fun word to say. "Little clouds of potato goodness" is the way to explain them to kids. Make an extra-big batch and freeze them for an easy weeknight dinner.

3 large baking potatoes, such as Idaho or russets (about 1¾ lbs/800 g)

1 large egg, at room temperature

1 tsp (5 mL) kosher salt

½ tsp (2.5 mL) freshly ground white pepper

Pinch of freshly grated nutmeg

½ cup (125 mL) freshly grated Parmesan

1½ cups (375 mL) all-purpose flour, plus more as needed

FREEZING GNOCCHI

Freeze gnocchi as soon as they are shaped. Arrange them in a single layer on a floured baking pan, and place the pan in the freezer (make sure it stays flat). Freeze until solid, about 3 hours. Gather the gnocchi into resealable freezer bags. Will keep in the freezer for 4 to 6 weeks.

Preheat the oven to 400°F (200°C).

Scrub the potatoes and prick all over with a fork. Place on a baking sheet, and bake for 30 minutes, or until a toothpick slides in easily.

The hotter the potatoes, the lighter the gnocchi, so wait until just cool enough to handle and work quickly. Cut the potatoes in half lengthwise. Use a folded tea towel or oven mitt to hold a potato half, and scoop the potato from the skin. Push the potatoes through a potato ricer into a large bowl. (You can also use a food mill fitted with the fine disc, but note that using a ricer will result in lighter gnocchi.)

In a small bowl, beat together the egg, salt, white pepper, and nutmeg.

Make a mound of the potatoes in the bowl, and form a well in the centre. Pour the egg mixture into the well. Quickly knead the potato and egg mixture together with both hands, gradually adding the Parmesan and enough of the flour—about 1½ cups (375 mL) to start—to form a smooth but slightly sticky dough. This should take no longer than 1 minute.

Wash and dry your hands. Lightly dust your hands and the work surface with flour. Turn out the dough onto the work surface and dust it with flour too. Have ready a floured or parchment paper–lined baking sheet for the shaped gnocchi.

Divide the dough into 6 equal pieces. Set aside the pieces you aren't working with, covering with a damp tea towel. Place one piece of dough in front of you, and pat it into a rough oblong shape. Using both hands, in a smooth back-and-forth rolling motion and exerting light downward pressure, form a ½-inch-diameter (1 cm) rope, flouring the dough and work surface if needed to keep it from sticking. (You may find it easier at first to work with a piece of dough that's half the size.)

...CONTINUED

... CONTINUED

Slice the ropes into ½-inch (1 cm) pieces with a bench scraper if you have one. Gently press down the centre to form little pillows. Set on the floured baking sheet. Continue forming gnocchi with the rest of the dough. Gnocchi must be cooked at this point; they can't be set aside, but you can also now freeze the gnocchi (see below).

COOK THE GNOCCHI: In a large pot, bring 6 quarts (6 L) of salted water to a vigorous boil over high heat.

Drop about half the gnocchi into the boiling water. Do not stir; just wait until they rise to the surface, about 4 minutes. Remove the gnocchi from the water with a slotted spoon or spider, and drain them well in a colander.

Continue with the remaining gnocchi. Refer to the following recipes for basil pesto and gorgonzola sauce for instructions on saucing and serving the gnocchi. Or simply sauté in butter and serve with plenty of shaved Parmesan.

HOW TO COOK FROZEN GNOCCHI

Cook directly from the freezer in plenty of boiling water or they will stick together. Bring 6 quarts (6 L) of salted water to a boil in a large pot. Boil one-half of the gnocchi at a time, making sure the other half stays in the freezer. Shake any excess flour from the frozen gnocchi, and stir gently as you add the gnocchi to the water. It's important that the water return to a boil as soon as possible; cover the pots if necessary. Wait until the gnocchi rises to the surface. Remove the gnocchi from the water with a slotted spoon or spider, and drain them well in a colander.

TO SERVE WITH GNOCCHI

Have ready ½ cup (125 mL) of shaved Parmesan to serve with the gnocchi. In a large nonstick skillet over medium heat, melt 2 tablespoons (30 mL) butter. After you've boiled and drained the gnocchi, add to the butter. Cook until golden brown and slightly crispy on the outside. Add the desired amount of pesto to coat the gnocchi. If the sauce is too dense or the gnocchi seem too dry, just add some of the gnocchi cooking water as you would with pasta water. Transfer to serving plates, and garnish with shaved Parmesan.

BASIL PESTO
Makes 1½ cups (375 mL) pesto

Pesto is the ideal Italian sauce when you want something different with pasta or chicken—or just about anything, really. We've tried (and loved) arugula pesto and parsley pesto, but we always come back to the classic basil version. There's just something that feels right about the way the basil plays off the buttery pine nuts, salty Parmesan, and licks of garlic. And it's perfect with gnocchi.

¼ cup (60 mL) toasted pine nuts
2 cups (500 mL) fresh basil, stems
    removed, chilled
5 cloves garlic, smashed and roughly
    chopped
¼ cup (60 mL) freshly grated Parmesan
    or pecorino Romano cheese
Zest of 1 lemon (optional)
Salt and freshly ground pepper
½ cup (125 mL) extra-virgin olive oil,
    plus more as needed

Place the bowl and blades of a food processor, as well as the pine nuts, in the refrigerator to chill for 30 minutes. (Keeping all the ingredients cold will ensure a bright green pesto.) Place all of the ingredients except the olive oil in the food processor, and blend until smooth. Use a spatula to scrape down the sides if necessary.

With the machine running, add the olive oil in a steady stream through the feed tube to emulsify. Season with more salt and freshly ground pepper, if necessary.

Keeps for 5 days in the refrigerator.

GORGONZOLA SAUCE
Makes about 3 cups (750 mL)

This is the ultimate in rich creamy cheese sauces, and it's tremendously versatile. We've even drizzled it over a sweet grilled veal chop. Gorgonzola is a salty cow's milk cheese with a sharp, blue-veined bite. But hey, any recipe with wine, cheese, and cream has got to be good, right?

1 cup (250 mL) heavy cream
1 cup (250 mL) white wine,
    preferably unoaked Chardonnay
½ cup (125 mL) chicken stock
½ cup (125 mL) crumbled gorgonzola,
1½ cups (375 mL) fresh spinach leaves
1½ tsp (7.5 mL) roughly chopped
    fresh rosemary
Shaved Parmesan for garnish

In a medium saucepan (or sauté pan if you're making pasta or gnocchi) over medium heat, add the cream, wine, and stock, and season with salt and freshly ground pepper. Bring to a simmer and reduce the mixture by half, about 10 minutes.

Add the gorgonzola, spinach, and rosemary, and stir to combine. Remove the pan from the heat.

When ready to serve, return the pan to medium heat for about 30 seconds to warm the sauce. Add the cooked gnocchi or pasta. Season with salt and freshly ground pepper, and if necessary adjust the consistency of sauce using leftover gnocchi or pasta water.

Plate and top the final dish with shaved Parmesan.

BOLOGNESE

Serves 4 to 6

This classic meat and tomato sauce is said to have originated, unsurprisingly, in the town of Bologna. It's a hearty sauce that sticks to your ribs—it includes beef *and* pork two-ways. Consider this a basic recipe that you can play with to make your own. Will you add rosemary? Red wine (heaven forbid!) instead of white? Entirely up to you. And remember, this is a great sauce for lasagna, too.

1½ cups (375 mL) roughly chopped fresh tomatoes, or canned tomatoes

2 Tbsp (30 mL) extra-virgin olive oil

½ lb (220 g) lean boneless stewing beef, cut into cubes

½ lb (220 g) boneless pork shoulder, cut into cubes

3 oz (85 g) pancetta, cut in ¼-inch (6 mm) dice (about ⅓ cup/80 mL)

1 medium Spanish onion, finely diced

2 large stalks celery, finely diced

1 medium carrot, peeled and finely diced

3 cloves garlic, finely chopped

1 cup (250 mL) dry white wine, preferably Sauvignon Blanc

Pinch of freshly grated nutmeg

1 bay leaf

¾ cup (185 mL) heavy cream

½ cup (125 mL) freshly chopped flat-leaf parsley, to serve

½ cup (125 mL) shaved Parmesan, to serve

Press the tomatoes through a food mill, using the fine disc, into a nonreactive bowl. Or process the tomatoes in a blender or food processor, then push the mixture through a sieve to remove the skin and seeds.

In a large skillet or enamelled cast iron pot or Dutch oven, heat the olive oil over medium-high. Brown the beef and pork pieces on all sides until deeply caramel coloured, turning as necessary. Transfer the meat to a large plate and set aside.

Add the pancetta to the pot, and cook for 2 minutes to render some of the fat. Add the onion, celery, carrot, and garlic to the pan, and sauté until the onions are translucent and carrots are browning. Add the reserved beef and pork (including any juices left on the plate), to the pot. Deglaze the pan with the wine, using a wooden spoon to scrape up the caramelized bits clinging to the bottom of the pan.

Add the strained tomatoes, and reduce the heat to low. Add the nutmeg and bay leaf, and season to taste with salt and freshly ground pepper. Cover and simmer, stirring occasionally, for 30 minutes, or until the meat is fork tender. When meat is tender, add the cream, and reduce, uncovered, for 20 minutes or until the sauce's thickness is to your liking.

Serve over your favourite pasta topped with parsley and Parmesan.

PASTA AGLIO E OLIO

Serves 4 to 6, and makes 1 cup (250 mL) olio santo

Aglio e olio simply means garlic and oil, but in this dish, the oil is usually infused with chili flakes. Have the oil on hand for midnight pasta cravings. It keeps in the fridge for two to three weeks.

OLIO SANTO

2 tsp (10 mL) red chili flakes

2 tsp (10 mL) finely chopped garlic

1 cup (250 mL) extra-virgin olive oil

FOR THE PASTA

1 Tbsp (15 mL) kosher salt, for the pasta water

1 lb (450 g) dried pasta

2 Tbsp (30 mL) olio santo, more to serve

1 cup (250 mL) fresh or frozen sweet peas

½ cup (125 mL) freshly grated Parmesan, plus more to serve

½ cup (125 mL) freshly chopped flat-leaf parsley, to serve (optional)

To make the olio santo, place the chili flakes and garlic into a 1-cup (250 mL) Mason jar. Pour the olive oil into a small saucepan. Set it over low, and heat until just warm, about 2 minutes. Pour the oil into the jar. Let it sit and infuse for 2 days in the refrigerator. (Keeps for 2 to 3 weeks in the fridge.) Remove from the fridge 30 minutes before using.

For the pasta, bring a large pot of cold water to a rolling boil over high heat, and add the salt. Add the pasta and cook, stirring occasionally, until al dente. Drain well in a colander.

While the pasta is cooking, heat the olio santo in a pot large enough to hold the pasta, such as a 12-inch (30 cm) sauté pan, over medium heat. Add the drained pasta. Add the peas and warm through, about 3 minutes. Add the Parmesan and some freshly cracked pepper.

Plate the pasta, drizzle with olio santo, and top with the grated Parmesan and parsley (if using).

WALNUT SAUCE

Makes 3½ cups (875 mL) walnut sauce

This may not be a pasta sauce you're familiar with, but it's certainly something to welcome into your repertoire. Also makes a decadent topping for grilled chicken, or a dip for crostini.

½ cup (125 mL) toasted
    pine nuts

2 cups (500 mL) toasted
    walnut halves

One ½-inch (1 cm)
    slice Italian bread

½ cup (125 mL) whole milk

½ clove garlic

½ cup (125 mL) freshly
    grated Parmesan

¾ cup (185 mL) extra-virgin
    olive oil

1 tsp (5 mL) fresh marjoram
    or oregano leaves

Toast the pine nuts in a dry skillet over low heat, shaking the pan occasionally to avoid burning, about 8 minutes. Watch closely, as pine nuts have a high oil content and can burn quite easily. Cool completely. In a separate larger skillet, toast the walnuts using the same method, except over medium heat. Cool completely.

In a small bowl, soak the bread in the milk for 5 to 10 minutes. Squeeze the excess milk from the bread, discarding the milk.

Place the walnuts, pine nuts, and garlic, plus a little salt, in a food processor. Add the bread. Process until you have a thick paste.

Transfer the mixture to a bowl. Using a wooden spoon, incorporate the Parmesan and olive oil. Lastly, add the marjoram (or oregano).

VEAL RAGÙ
Serves 8

A relatively tough cut of meat becomes melt-in-your-mouth after four hours of gentle braising. We match it with the large noodle pappardelle to create a comforting and rustic meal. Serve with a big green salad.

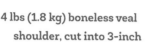

4 lbs (1.8 kg) boneless veal shoulder, cut into 3-inch (8 cm) chunks

¼ cup (60 mL) all-purpose flour

½ cup (125 mL) extra-virgin olive oil, divided

1 large Spanish onion, finely chopped

4 cloves garlic, finely chopped

1½ tsp (7.5 mL) ground coriander

1½ tsp (7.5 mL) ground fennel

1 Tbsp (15 mL) tomato paste

1½ cups (375 mL) dry white wine, preferably Italian

4 cups (1 L) veal stock (or chicken stock)

1 sprig fresh rosemary

2 lbs (900 g) fresh pappardelle or 1½ lbs (670 g) dried pappardelle

1 Tbsp (15 mL) kosher salt, for the pasta water

1 cup (250 mL) shaved or grated Parmesan

2 Tbsp (30 mL) freshly chopped chives

Season the veal with salt and freshly ground pepper and dust with the flour, tapping off the excess.

Preheat a large enamelled cast iron pot or Dutch oven over medium-high heat. Add ¼ cup (60 mL) of the olive oil. When the oil is hot, add the veal and brown on all sides until caramelized, turning as necessary, about 12 minutes in total. Remove the pot from the heat and transfer the veal to a plate.

Add the remaining ¼ cup (60 mL) of oil to the same pot. Stir in the onion, garlic, coriander, and fennel, and cook over low heat for 5 minutes or until onion is soft and translucent.

Stir in the tomato paste, and then the wine, and let it simmer until reduced to ⅓ cup (80 mL), about 5 minutes. Add the stock and rosemary and bring to a boil over medium-high heat, then reduce the heat to a gentle simmer.

Return the veal (and any juices left on the plate) to the pot. Partially cover, and cook over low heat, stirring occasionally, until very tender, about 2 hours. Remove the pot from the heat. Let the veal sit (and continue to absorb the flavour of the braising liquid), until the veal is cool enough to handle.

Remove the meat from the pot, and shred it using a fork. Return the sauce to a simmer over medium heat until slightly reduced, about 10 minutes. Stir in the meat, and keep the ragù warm.

For the pasta, bring a large pot of cold water to a rolling boil over high heat, and add the salt. Add the pappardelle and cook, stirring occasionally, until al dente, about 3 minutes for fresh pasta. (For dried, the package should offer an approximate time.) Drain well in a colander.

Add the pasta to the ragù, and toss over low heat until the pasta is coated with the sauce. Serve with plenty of Parmesan and garnish with chives.

BUCATINI WITH SEAFOOD
Serves 4

The best part of a seafood sauce (apart from the great taste) is how simple and fast it is to make. This recipe calls for a crisp Pinot Grigio. Whenever you can, try to cook with the same wine you'll serve at dinner so the flavours on the plate mirror the flavours in your glass. Bucatini is a long hollow cylindrical pasta that sort of looks like a straw. Any tube-shaped pasta will do in a pinch.

½ lb (220 g) fresh mussels

½ lb (220 g) clams

½ lb (220 g) large shrimp
    (10/12 count)

½ lb (220 g) sea scallops,
    quartered

½ lb (220 g) skin-on red
    snapper fillet (scaled)

¼ cup (60 mL) extra-virgin
    olive oil

1 large Spanish onion,
    cut in medium dice

4 cloves garlic,
    finely chopped

2 tsp (10 mL) red chili flakes

1½ cups (375 mL) dry white
    wine, preferably Pinot
    Grigio

1 cup (250 mL) bottled
    or canned clam juice

1 cup (250 mL) diced red
    and yellow tomatoes
    (medium dice)

1 cup (250 mL) roughly
    chopped fresh flat-leaf
    parsley, divided

1½ lbs (670 g) fresh bucatini
    or 1 lb (450 g)
    dried bucatini

1 Tbsp (15 mL) kosher salt,
    for the pasta water

Good-quality extra-virgin
    olive oil, to finish

¾ cup (185 mL) shaved
    Parmesan, to serve

1 lemon, cut into
    wedges, to serve

Make sure that the mussels and clams are all closed tightly; lightly tap on a hard surface the ones that aren't, and see if it closes. If not, discard. Scrub and debeard the mussels, and scrub the clams. Peel and devein the shrimp; quarter the sea scallops; and remove the pin bones from the snapper, and then cut into 1½-inch (4 cm) pieces.

Place a very large (16-inch/40 cm) skillet over medium-high heat. (If you don't have a skillet that size, use 2.) Add the olive oil, and heat for 30 seconds. Add the onions, garlic, and chili flakes, and sauté for 1 minute.

Add the clams and mussels, season with salt and freshly ground pepper, and cook for 1 minute. Then add the scallops and shrimp, and cook until the scallops are golden on one side and shrimp are bright pink. Turn them over. Add the snapper skin side down, and cook for

1 minute. Turn over the snapper and sear the other side until golden.

Deglaze with the wine and clam juice. Add the tomatoes and half of the parsley, cover, and reduce the heat to low. Cook until the clams and mussels open. If there are some that don't open, discard them.

While the sauce is cooking, prepare the bucatini. Bring a large pot of cold water to a rolling boil over high heat, and add the salt. Add the bucatini and cook, stirring occasionally, until al dente, about 3 minutes for fresh pasta. (For dried, the package should offer an approximate time.) Drain well in a colander.

Plate the pasta, and place the seafood on top. Drizzle with extra-virgin olive oil, and top with the Parmesan and the remaining parsley. Serve with a lemon wedge.

FUSILLI WITH SPINACH AND RICOTTA
Serves 3

Spinach and ricotta usually play a supporting role in a classic lasagna, but here they take centre stage. Ricotta (which means "recooked") is made from milk whey left over from the making of other cheeses. The rich, creamy sauce clings perfectly to fusilli, a little cork-screw-shaped pasta. And remember: for mysterious taste bud reasons, nutmeg is essential to the dish.

1 cup (250 mL) fresh ricotta cheese

1 cup (250 mL) half-and-half or light cream

½ tsp (2.5 mL) freshly grated nutmeg

2 Tbsp (30 mL) extra-virgin olive oil

4 small green onions, thinly sliced on the bias

1 lb (450 g) fresh spinach, washed and dried well, stems removed

2 Tbsp (30 mL) unsalted butter

1 lb (450 g) dried fusilli or 1½ lbs (670 g) fresh fusilli

1 Tbsp (15 mL) kosher salt, for the pasta water

½ cup (125 mL) freshly grated Parmesan, more to serve

1 to 2 lemons, cut into wedges, to serve

In a small bowl, stir together the ricotta, half-and-half (or light cream), and nutmeg until smooth.

In a very large sauté pan, heat the olive oil over medium-high heat. Add the green onions and cook, stirring, until softened, about 1 minute. Add the spinach along with the butter. Cook for 1 minute, or until the spinach is slightly wilted. Stir in the ricotta mixture, and season with salt and freshly ground pepper. Reduce the heat to medium-low, and simmer for 4 minutes. Remove the pan from the heat.

For the pasta, bring a large pot of cold water to a rolling boil over high heat, and add the salt. Add the fusilli and cook, stirring occasionally, until al dente. (For dried pasta, the package should offer an approximate time; for fresh, start checking after 3 minutes.) Drain well in a colander, reserving ½ cup (125 mL) of the pasta cooking water. Return the pot to the stove.

Return the pasta to the pot, and place over low heat. Add the spinach-ricotta mixture and enough of the reserved pasta water to make a sauce that lightly coats the pasta, tossing the pasta thoroughly. Season with salt and plenty of freshly ground pepper. Remove the pot from the heat, and stir in the grated cheese.

Transfer the pasta to a warm serving platter or individual bowls, and serve with lemon wedges.

ORECCHIETTE WITH SAUSAGE AND LEEKS

Serves 4

Orecchiette means "small ear," and this pasta's shape is a perfect little cup for holding the sweet gravy-like sauce that comes from cooking sweet Italian sausage with gentle leeks and tangy shallots then finished with Parmesan, cream and Dijon mustard. To keep the peas firm and crunchy, wait till the end before adding.

2 Tbsp (30 mL) extra-virgin olive oil

12 oz (340 g) sweet Italian sausage, casings removed, crumbled

2 large leeks, white and light green parts only, cut into ¼-inch (6 mm) slices

2 Tbsp (30 mL) sliced shallots (¼-inch/ 6 mm slices)

½ cup (125 mL) white wine, preferably Pinot Grigio

¾ cup (185 mL) heavy cream

2 Tbsp (30 mL) Dijon mustard

1 lb (450 g) dried orecchiette

1 Tbsp (15 mL) kosher salt, for the pasta water

1 cup (250 mL) frozen sweet peas, defrosted and drained, or fresh peas (parcook if using fresh)

1 Tbsp (15 mL) of butter

½ cup (125 mL) freshly grated Parmesan, plus more to serve, if you like

In a large skillet, heat the olive oil over medium-high heat. Cook the sausage, breaking up any lumps, until it starts to turn golden on one side, about 5 minutes.

Add the leeks and cook, stirring, until soft, about 4 minutes. Stir in the shallots and cook for 1 minute. Deglaze with the wine, and add the cream and Dijon. Stir to incorporate, and season with black pepper. Keep warm while pasta is cooking.

For the pasta, bring a large pot of cold water to a rolling boil over high heat, and add the salt. Add the orecchiette and cook, stirring occasionally, until al dente. Drain well in a colander.

Add the pasta to the sausage and leek sauce, and toss well. Add the peas just to heat through.

Remove the pot from the heat, and add the butter and Parmesan; toss well. Season with salt and freshly ground pepper, to taste. Transfer to a warmed serving platter or individual bowls. Serve immediately, with more grated cheese on the side, if you like.

RISOTTO

Serves 4

What can we say about risotto? It's a classic comfort food made rich and creamy by the starchy arborio rice (please, no other rice will do) kissed by pancetta, shocked by cold white wine, sopped in hot chicken stock, and slathered in Parmesan. Take your time making this dish. Don't skip a step to try and hurry it up. The rice needs to slowly absorb the chicken stock to achieve the creaminess you want. Tip: You know you're in a so-so Italian restaurant when they can bring you risotto in five minutes. Where's the love?

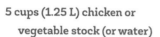

5 cups (1.25 L) chicken or vegetable stock (or water)

1 Tbsp (15 mL) extra-virgin olive oil

½ cup (125 mL) diced pancetta, about 4 oz (110 g)

1 medium onion, finely diced (about 1 cup/250 mL)

2 cups (500 mL) arborio rice

1 cup (250 mL) white wine, preferably Sauvignon Blanc

2 cups (500 mL) sweet peas

½ tsp (2.5 mL) coarsely ground black pepper

½ cup (125 mL) freshly grated Parmesan or pecorino Romano cheese, plus more to serve

2 Tbsp (30 mL) freshly chopped parsley

1 Tbsp (15 mL) butter

In a medium saucepan, bring the stock to a simmer over medium heat, and keep it at a simmer.

Heat the olive oil in a wide pot over medium-high heat. Add the pancetta and cook to render the fat, about 3 minutes. Add the onions, stir to coat, and cook until it softens, about 2 minutes. Add the rice and cook for about 90 seconds, stirring constantly to coat all of the grains and to avoid sticking.

Add the wine. Cook, stirring frequently, until the wine evaporates (you'll be able smell the alcohol burning off), about 90 seconds.

Add 1 cup (250 mL) of the stock and continue cooking, stirring well and often, until the rice has absorbed all of the liquid, about 4 minutes. Do this 3 to 4 more times, waiting after each addition of stock until the rice has absorbed all the liquid (16 to 20 minutes in total). Taste the rice; it should be al dente.

Add the peas and the black pepper. Stir continuously for 2 minutes, or until the rice has absorbed most of the liquid. The peas should be cooked through but still bright green and crunchy.

Remove the pan from the heat. Add the Parmesan, parsley, and butter. Season with salt and freshly ground pepper to taste. Serve immediately, sprinkled with more cheese.

MARINATED CHICKEN ALLA GRIGLIA WITH ROASTED POTATOES AND ONIONS

Serves 2 to 4

Get your butcher to remove the backbone, or cut it out yourself using kitchen shears. Just cut along each side of the bone (the bone is great for making stock). You can then flatten out—or "spatchcock"—the bird, which makes for even grilling. Whole chickens can otherwise be challenging to grill; they can dry out, burn, and remain uncooked, usually all at once! But this chicken stays juicy and tender while the skin becomes perfectly crisp. Serve with roast spuds and a lemony kale salad.

ROASTED GARLIC

1 head garlic

Drizzle of extra-virgin olive oil

1 sprig fresh thyme

About 2 Tbsp (30 mL) red wine, preferably Cabernet Sauvignon

MARINADE

½ cup (125 mL) rice vinegar or white wine vinegar

½ cup (125 mL) extra-virgin olive oil

1 lemon, thinly sliced

2 Tbsp (30 mL) freshly chopped rosemary

1 Tbsp (15 mL) fresh oregano leaves

1 Tbsp (15 mL) fresh thyme leaves

1 tsp (5 mL) red chili flakes

2 tsp (10 mL) granulated sugar

1 tsp (5 mL) kosher salt

1 tsp (5 mL) coarsely ground black pepper

FOR THE CHICKEN

1 whole chicken, about 5 lbs (2.25 kg), backbone removed

1 lemon, cut into ¼-inch (6 mm) slices

Extra-virgin olive oil for grilling

ROASTED POTATOES AND ONIONS

2 lbs (900 g) baby potatoes (about 20)

1 Spanish onion, cut into wedges

1 Tbsp (15 mL) fresh thyme leaves

1 Tbsp (15 mL) extra-virgin olive oil

. . . CONTINUED

ROASTED GARLIC: Preheat the oven to 300°F (150°C).

Using a sharp knife, cut off the tops of the heads of garlic just enough to expose the cloves. Pierce all over with the tines of a fork. Place in a small ovenproof pan. Drizzle with olive oil, and then with the wine. Top with the thyme sprigs and sprinkle with black pepper (no salt as it will draw out the moisture). Cover the pan with aluminum foil and seal well.

Roast until very soft when poked, about 35 minutes. Let cool.

MARINADE: Squeeze out the soft cloves of the garlic, and mash with the side of a chef's knife. Transfer to a bowl with the rest of the marinade ingredients, and mix well.

FOR THE CHICKEN: Place the chicken breast side down in a large baking dish or glass container. Open up the chicken to find a notch in the middle in between the breasts, and make a cut about ¼ inch (6 mm) deep. Then push upward and bend open the chicken to expose the breastbone. The chicken should now be flat. Pour the marinade all over the chicken. Cover with plastic wrap and marinate in the fridge for at least 8 hours, or overnight.

ROASTED POTATOES AND ONIONS: Preheat the oven to 400°F (200°C).

Place the potatoes in a large pot of cold water set over high heat, and add generous amount of kosher salt. Bring to a boil, then reduce to medium-low. Simmer the potatoes for 10 minutes, or until cooked but slightly firm when inserted with a knife. Drain the potatoes and let cool.

Cut the potatoes in half, and place in a large bowl. Add the onions, thyme, and olive oil, and season with salt and freshly ground pepper. Toss to coat evenly.

Transfer to a baking sheet, placing the potatoes cut side down. Roast for 10 to 15 minutes or until the cut side is crispy and golden. Stir the potatoes and onions, and continue to roast until onions are soft and slightly caramelized, 5 to 7 more minutes. Transfer to a serving platter.

GRILL THE CHICKEN: Preheat the grill to medium, then clean and oil the grill grates to prevent sticking.

Transfer the chicken to a plate to drain off some of the marinade, but make sure not to wipe off the herbs (which are delicious charred right on the skin). Season with salt and freshly ground pepper.

Place the chicken breast side down and grill without moving until nice crisp char marks appear, about 5 minutes. Using tongs, carefully turn the chicken 45 degrees. Cook until the skin is golden brown and crispy, then flip.

Reduce the heat to medium-low, and continue to cook for at least 14 minutes. Insert an instant-read thermometer in the thickest part of the chicken; it should read 165°F to 170°F (74°C–77°C).

Transfer the chicken onto a serving platter and let rest, covered loosely with aluminum foil. Meanwhile, increase the heat of the grill to medium-high. Drizzle the lemon slices with olive oil and place on the grill. Cook for 1 minute or until deep char marks develop. Turn over to grill the other side.

Carve the chicken, and serve with the charred lemons and roasted potatoes and onions.

GRILLED PARMESAN POLENTA

Serves 4 to 6

Someone described polenta as boiled cornmeal. *This* is the way polenta is meant to be served: first gently simmered into a sweet, creamy rich porridge and set till firm, sliced and grilled till visually stunning with deep recessed grill marks playing off the natural golden hue of the cornmeal. Now *that's* polenta! So simple, so good. Try it creamy right out of the pot or put it into the fridge to firm up and then grill it in slices.

4½ cups (1.125 L) water

1½ tsp (7.5 mL) kosher salt

2 cups (500 mL) fine or semi-fine polenta cornmeal (or medium-ground yellow cornmeal), not quick-cooking

2 Tbsp (30 mL) butter

½ cup (125 mL) freshly grated Parmesan

1 Tbsp (15 mL) extra-virgin olive oil, for grilling

Line a 9- by 5-inch (23 × 12 cm) loaf pan with parchment paper.

In a medium saucepan, bring the water to a boil over high heat, then reduce to a simmer at medium-low heat and add the salt.

Using a whisk, beat continuously as you slowly pour in the cornmeal, keeping the water at a simmer. Switch to a wooden spoon and continue stirring until thick, about 8 minutes.

Remove the pan from the heat. Add the butter and Parmesan, season with salt and freshly ground pepper to taste, then stir to incorporate. Place in the parchment-lined pan and refrigerate until set, about 1 hour.

Remove the polenta from the loaf pan. Cut it into ½-inch-thick (1 cm) slices, then cut each slice diagonally to create a triangle.

Preheat the grill to medium, then clean and oil the grill grates to prevent sticking.

Drizzle to lightly coat the polenta with oil, and season to taste with more salt and freshly ground pepper. Grill the polenta until nice golden char marks develop, about 2 minutes. Turn over and repeat for the other side. Serve immediately.

POLENTA FRIES
Serves 4 to 6

Polenta fries are an excellent alternative to the old spud—and an alternative to sweet potato fries, which we find can get soggy. These crisp up beautifully and retain a buttery smooth interior. Pile them up next to a juicy bone-in rib steak. Follow the previous recipe through to the step where you chill the loaf pan in the fridge.

1 recipe polenta (page 118), chilled for 1 hour
Vegetable oil for deep-frying, about 4 cups (1 L)
2 Tbsp (30 mL) freshly chopped parsley, for garnish
½ cup (125 mL) shaved Parmesan, for garnish

Remove the polenta from the loaf pan. Cut the polenta into ½-inch (1 cm) slices, then cut into ½-inch (1 cm) batons.

Line a baking sheet with paper towels. In a heavy-bottomed pot or wok over medium-high, heat the oil to 375°F (191°C).

In small batches, gently lower the polenta into the hot oil. Deep-fry until slightly brown and crispy. Remove with a slotted spoon or spider, and drain on the paper towels. Repeat with the remaining polenta.

Place on a serving platter sprinkled with parsley and Parmesan.

VEAL SALTIMBOCCA
Serves 3

Saltimbocca literally translates to "jumps in the mouth." When you consider the tantalizing ingredients in this recipe, it's easy to see why. Salty prosciutto and earthy sage flavour thin strips of lean veal perfumed in a white wine bath. And it's *so* easy to make. Read on.

6 slices veal scaloppini,
  about 9 oz (255 g)
1 Tbsp (15 mL) roughly
  chopped fresh sage
6 slices prosciutto
1 cup (250 mL) fresh spinach
  leaves (stems removed)
2 Tbsp (30 mL) butter
1 Tbsp (15 mL) extra-virgin
  olive oil
1 cup (250 mL) Marsala wine
½ cup (125 mL) heavy
  cream or 2 Tbsp (30 mL)
  cold butter
6 round toothpicks

Place 1 veal scaloppini between 2 sheets of waxed paper or plastic wrap. Flatten to a ⅛-inch (3 mm) thickness using a meat pounder (a flat meat pounder and not one with a toothed surface), a rolling pin, or the bottom of a pot. Repeat with the remaining veal.

Lay 1 piece flat on your work surface. Season with black pepper, drape with a slice of prosciutto, and place one-sixth of the sage and spinach evenly over the top the prosciutto. Roll up like a pinwheel and secure with a toothpick. Repeat with the remaining veal.

Preheat a large skillet over medium-high heat, and melt the butter in the olive oil. Sear the saltimbocca until all sides are golden brown, about 5 minutes.

Transfer the veal to a dish and set aside. Pour off the excess fat from the skillet.

Add the Marsala to the skillet and bring to a simmer over medium-low heat, scraping up any of the browned bits at the bottom of the pan. Simmer until the liquid is reduced by half. Whisk in the cream (or the cold butter), then season with salt and freshly ground pepper. Add the scaloppini, and toss to heat through and to coat with the sauce.

Remove the toothpicks from the scaloppini, and slice into ¾-inch (2 cm) rounds. Serve draped with the sauce.

SHORT RIBS IN RED WINE

Serves 4 to 6

Short ribs are a good reason to get to know your butcher on a first-name basis. Call ahead so they can set some aside for you. Now, slow braising isn't uniquely Italian, but when you do it with a nice Barolo wine and crushed tomatoes, and top the ribs with pine nuts and Parmesan . . . well, *that's* Italian!

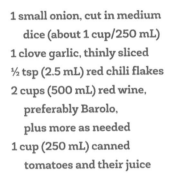

4 bone-in short ribs
(about 3 lbs/1.4 kg),
cut into thirds
1 Tbsp (15 mL) kosher salt
½ tsp (2.5 mL) freshly
cracked black pepper
3 Tbsp (45 mL) extra-virgin
olive oil
½ cup (125 mL) roughly
diced pancetta, about
4 oz (110 g)

1 small onion, cut in medium
dice (about 1 cup/250 mL)
1 clove garlic, thinly sliced
½ tsp (2.5 mL) red chili flakes
2 cups (500 mL) red wine,
preferably Barolo,
plus more as needed
1 cup (250 mL) canned
tomatoes and their juice

FOR THE TOPPING
¼ cup (60 mL) pine nuts,
roughly chopped
1 Tbsp (15 mL) extra-virgin
olive oil
¼ cup (60 mL) breadcrumbs
2 tsp (10 mL) dried oregano
½ tsp (2.5 mL) coarsely
ground black pepper
2 Tbsp (30 mL) freshly
chopped parsley
2 Tbsp (30 mL) freshly
grated Parmesan

Preheat the oven to 325°F (160°C).

Season the short ribs on all sides with the salt and pepper. Preheat a large ovenproof enamalled cast iron pot or Dutch oven over medium heat, then add the olive oil. Cook the short ribs until all surfaces are a deep caramel brown, turning as necessary. Transfer the ribs to a plate and set aside.

Add the pancetta to the pot, and cook for 3 minutes or until golden brown and most of the fat has rendered. Add the onion and cook until it softens, about 1 minute. Stir in the garlic and the chili flakes, and cook for 1 minute.

Deglaze the pan with the wine, and use a wooden spoon to scrape up all the brown bits that are stuck to the bottom of the pot. Simmer the wine for 1 minute. Return the short ribs (and any juices left on the plate) to the pot.

. . . CONTINUED

Crush the tomatoes over a bowl with your hands, then add to the pot along with their juice. The liquid should almost cover the ribs; add more wine if necessary.

Bring the mixture to a simmer, cover, and transfer the pot to the oven. Cook for 2 hours or until the ribs are fork tender. Remove the lid, and cook another 30 minutes or so to reduce the sauce by half.

Make the topping while the short ribs cook in the oven. Toast the pine nuts in a dry skillet over low heat, shaking the pan occasionally to avoid burning, about 8 minutes. Watch closely, as pine nuts have a high oil content and can burn quite easily.

Add the olive oil and breadcrumbs and continue to cook, watching closely and stirring constantly, over low heat, until a golden toasted brown. Add the oregano and pepper. Cook a few seconds longer, then remove the skillet from the heat. Let cool. Stir in the parsley and Parmesan.

When the ribs are done, let rest for 15 minutes in the flavour-ful liquid. Remove the ribs from the pot, and place on a plate loosely covered with aluminum foil.

Remove some of the fat from the sauce—this step is optional, but it does makes the sauce taste better and less greasy. Tip the pot, and using a ladle, move aside the meat and slowly press down on the sauce so that it fills with only the clear fat. There will be at least 2 tablespoons (30 mL) of fat.

Place the pot over medium heat, and season to taste with pepper. Add ½ cup (125 mL) of water to the sauce if it's too thick.

Place 3 to 4 pieces on a serving plate, and top with the sauce. Sprinkle a generous amount of the topping over the ribs.

PORCHETTA
Serves a very large group (15 or more)

Going back centuries, and across all cultures, people have had to find ways to use lesser, tougher cuts of meat. Typically this is done by marinating and braising. In Italy, they came up with something called porchetta—a sweet, tender, slow-roasted pork belly. The four-hour roasting time crisps the skin to achieve what's known as "crackle." Our little secret to get it "crispified" is to rub some baking powder into the skin before it goes into the oven. Definitely *not* a diet dish, and oh-so-good.

1 whole pork belly, boneless
   with the rind on, about
   12 lbs (5.4 kg)

2 Tbsp (30 mL) black
   peppercorns

2 Tbsp (30 mL) fennel seeds

12 cloves garlic

Zest of 1 orange

Zest of 1 lemon

1 Tbsp (15 mL) red
   chili flakes

3 Tbsp (45 mL) finely
   chopped fresh rosemary,
   sage, thyme, and oregano

1 Tbsp (15 mL) kosher salt

2 tsp (10 mL) baking powder
   mixed with 2 Tbsp (30 mL)
   kosher salt,
   for the crackle

EQUIPMENT

Kitchen twine

Large roasting
   pan with a rack

Place the pork belly skin side down on a large cutting board. Using a sharp chef's knife, score the flesh at an angle using strokes about 1 inch (2.5 cm) apart. Rotate knife 90 degrees and score again, creating a diamond pattern in the flesh.

Toast the peppercorns and fennel seeds in a small skillet over medium-high heat until lightly browned and aromatic, about 2 minutes. Transfer to a spice grinder (or coffee grinder set aside for spices) and grind until roughly crushed. Add the garlic, orange and lemon zest, and chili flakes, and blend. Transfer to a small bowl, and stir in the herbs and a drizzle of olive oil to form a rough paste.

Season the pork liberally with the salt, then rub the paste all over the top of the belly, making sure to get into all the cracks and crevices.

Cut 5 to 6 lengths of kitchen twine long enough to go around the pork belly. Roll the belly into a tight log and leave it seam side down, and set it aside. Lay the kitchen twine on the cutting board at 1-inch (2.5 cm) intervals. Place the belly seam side down on top of the twine.

Working from the outside toward the centre, tie up the roast tightly. At this point, if you think the roast is too large and unwieldy, carefully slice it in half with a sharp chef's knife.

Rub the baking powder and salt mixture over the entire surface of porchetta. This will help in the blistering of the skin for the treasured crackling. Wrap tightly in plastic wrap, and keep refrigerated overnight at the very least, and up to 3 days.

Adjust the rack to the lower-middle position of the oven, and preheat to 300°F (150°C).

...CONTINUED

Place the pork on the rack in the roasting pan. Roast, basting with the pan drippings every 30 minutes, for about 4 hours or until the internal temperature of pork reaches 160°F (71°C) (or 150°F/66°C if you desire porchetta to be medium instead of medium-well).

If the skin hasn't completely crisped up, increase the oven to 400°F (200°C). It may take up to 15 minutes for the skin to be completely crispy and blistered; watch closely. (You can also remove the roast from the oven, letting it rest tented with foil for up to 1 hour before finishing it in the oven to crisp up the skin.)

Remove the roast from the oven, transfer to a plate, and cover loosely with aluminum foil. Let rest for at least 20 minutes before slicing. Slice into 1-inch-thick (2.5 cm) rounds using a serrated knife, and serve.

TO SERVE WITH ROASTED POTATOES AND SHALLOTS

Blanch some potatoes in boiling salted water until almost done. Slice in half. Roast potatoes and peeled shallots on a baking sheet after the roast is done, drizzled and tossed with the pork drippings and seasoned with salt and freshly ground pepper. Roast in a 400°F (200°C) oven, turning every 10 minutes, until the potatoes are crisp and the shallots are soft, about 20 minutes.

RAPINI WITH GOAT CHEESE, ONIONS, AND PINE NUTS

Serves 4

Rapini, also known as broccoli rabe, has some of the bitterness of broccoli (a good thing). The longer stems, smaller florets, and leaves all stand up well to sautéing. Sweet sun-dried tomatoes, buttery pine nuts, and creamy goat cheese provide a balance of flavours in this time-honoured side dish.

2 bunch rapini
   (broccoli raab)
4 Tbsp (45 mL) pine nuts
3 Tbsp (30 mL) extra-virgin
   olive oil
1 Vidalia onion, thinly sliced
1 clove garlic, finely chopped
½ tsp (2.5 mL) red chili flakes
8 sun-dried tomatoes
   in oil, julienned
4 Tbsp (30 mL) fresh
   goat cheese
Juice of 1 lemon (optional)

To toast the pine nuts, place a medium pan over low heat. Add the pine nuts, and shake the pan regularly to avoid burning. Cook until a light golden brown. Watch closely, as pine nuts have a high oil content and can burn quite easily. Remove the pan from the heat. Set aside.

Have ready a bowl of ice water. Boil a large pot of water over high heat, and add a generous amount of salt. While waiting for the water to boil, cut off the bottoms of the rapini stems, remove any large, bruised leaves, and wash well. Blanch the rapini for 1 minute, until the leaves have softened but the stems are still nice and firm. Remove the rapini using tongs or a spider, and place in the bowl of ice water to stop the cooking process and help keep its vibrant green colour.

Heat the olive oil in a large sauté pan over medium heat. Add the onions and sauté until soft and translucent, about 5 minutes. Stir in the garlic and chili flakes. Add the whole pieces of rapini and the sun-dried tomatoes, and generous pinches of salt and freshly ground pepper. Increase the heat to medium-high heat and cook about 2 minutes.

Transfer the mixture to a large serving platter. Right before serving, crumble the goat cheese over the top. (You don't want it to let it stand too long, or the cheese will get runny or melt completely.) Add the lemon juice, if using.

Sprinkle the pine nuts over the rapini and serve immediately.

SEMIFREDDO
Serves 8 to 10

The classic Italian dessert, but with regular chocolate *and* Nutella. There are quite a few steps here, so spread it out over two nights or a long Sunday afternoon. Invite the whole family to get involved in the making.

1 cup (250 mL) cold
    heavy cream
4 large egg yolks,
    at room temperature
3 Tbsp (45 mL) whole milk
½ cup (120 mL) granulated
    sugar, divided
5 oz (140 g) dark chocolate
    (70% to 85%), finely
    chopped, or finely ground
    in a food processor
½ cup (125 mL) Nutella
2 large egg whites,
    at room temperature
½ tsp (2.5 mL) cream of tartar
1 Tbsp (15 mL) brandy or
    coffee liqueur (optional)
½ cup (125 mL) crushed
    toasted hazelnuts
    (see the tip on page 63)

Chill a medium-size metal bowl and the beaters of an electric hand mixer in the freezer until very cold.

Line the bottom and long sides of a 9- by 5-inch (23 × 12 cm) loaf pan with a piece of plastic wrap that's at least 20 inches (50 cm) long so that you will have a 4-inch (10 cm) overhang on the long sides. (This is to help pull out the semifreddo from the pan in the end.) Smooth the plastic along the sides and into the corners.

Remove the bowl and the beaters from the freezer, and whip the cream with the mixer on medium-high speed just until firm peaks form, about 1 minute. Cover and refrigerate. Clean and dry beaters.

MAKE ZABAGLIONE: Fill a 4-quart (4 L) saucepan with about 2 inches (5 cm) of water. Bring to a boil over high heat, then reduce the heat to maintain a gentle simmer.

Place the egg yolks, milk, and ¼ cup (60 mL) of the sugar in a medium-size metal bowl. Set it over the pot of simmering water, making sure the bottom of the bowl doesn't touch the water. Using the electric hand mixer, beat on medium speed until the zabaglione is thick, almost doubled in volume, and the beaters leave a trail when you lift them, about 5 minutes. You'll need to scrape down the sides of the bowl with a heatproof spatula while you beat the mixture. Remove the bowl from on top of the pot.

In another bowl that fits on top of the pot, warm the chocolate and Nutella over the simmering water until almost melted. Fold this chocolate mixture into the zabaglione until melted and smooth. Set aside. Clean and dry the beaters.

. . . CONTINUED

MAKE MERINGUE: Return the pot of water to the heat and maintain the water at a gentle simmer; you may need to add more water at this point.

In a large metal bowl set over the simmering water, place the egg whites, the remaining ¼ cup (60 mL) sugar, and the cream of tartar, plus a pinch of salt. Using an electric hand mixer, beat on medium speed, occasionally scraping down the sides of the bowl with a clean heatproof spatula, until light, fluffy, and shiny, about 3 minutes. Remove the bowl from the pan and continue beating until the meringue is very thick and billowy, about 2 minutes more.

Use the spatula to gently fold the zabaglione into the meringue. Remove the whipped cream from the fridge and gently fold it in until no streaks remain. Whisk in the brandy or coffee liqueur, if using.

Scrape the mixture into the prepared pan. Smooth the top with an offset spatula, scraping off any excess to create a level surface. Wrap the overhanging plastic over the top to cover the loaf pan. Freeze for at least 6 hours and up to 3 days.

Unwrap the plastic from the top of the pan. Invert the pan onto a cutting board or serving platter. Lift off the pan, holding the overhanging plastic down on one side and then the other. Peel off the plastic wrap. If the semifreddo looks wrinkled from the plastic wrap, warm a long knife or small offset spatula under hot running water, wipe the blade dry, and run it over the surface to smooth it out.

To serve, cut the semifreddo into 1-inch-thick (2.5 cm) slices, and garnish with the hazelnuts.

INDIA

Vijaya Selvaraju

Chennai, or Madras as it was once known, in Tamil Nadu, is one of the most vibrant cities in the world. It is home to approximately 4.5 million people, has one of the longest beaches in the world, and is the headquarters of the booming film industry known as Kollywood.

Chennai is where I was born, but Toronto is where I grew up. So my perception of (and great affection for) Chennai comes largely from the family vacations that we used to take. We'd walk through the open-air markets with all the fresh produce on display. Vendors, usually elderly women or *ayyas*, would sit by their piles of mangoes, freshly caught fish, and leafy local greens and call to passersby, proudly describing their goods. I loved the hustle and bustle. It's where I learned the art of how to shop from my mom: Feel the mango—does it slightly give when you press your thumb into it? Smell the fish—does it remind you of the ocean? Shake the greens—do they stand tall and crisp? Fruits, vegetables, grains, and meats would all undergo tests before making it into our basket. On our way home we'd think of all the delicious possibilities, and by dinnertime there'd be a spread ready for all our family to dig into. These kinds of adventures would continue through our travels in southern India, in cities like Madurai, my mom's hometown, and Karaikal, where my dad was born.

We'd return home and our suitcases would be packed with spices, snacks, and trinkets to help us overcome the post-India blues and make the transition back to regular life bearable. My mom would open her *masala dhaba*, a stainless-steel box with small round containers for storing spices, and replenish them with her new treasures. Our house would continue to fill with the aromas of our motherland.

While we enjoyed experimenting with many different cuisines, Indian food was a constant in our household. As a child, I would hold onto my mom's *salwar kameez* and try to squeeze my way into her kitchen and help out however I could. (I still do!) I'd top and tail green beans, peel shrimp, rinse rice—tasks that my small, nimble fingers were good at and that my mom trusted me with. I would watch my mom grind rice and dal in a stone grinder to make idli, the steamed dumpling. Though I was never allowed

to get anywhere near the idli machine, I was encouraged to watch, and to feel the batter at different stages.

And so began my education in Indian cuisine. Spice pastes were ground, fish was fried, dals soaked, fritters formed. My mom started to give me tasks that increased in difficulty. I was ten when I learned how to make puffy chapatis and crisp *bhajjis*. I discovered all of the magical ingredients that went into my mom's masalas, and was sworn never to tell another soul! These were recipes passed down through generations.

So many dishes, so little time. India is diverse with different landscapes and different climates. Each region, state, city, and village (and maybe even household) has a different cuisine. And we were lucky to have friends from all over the country that would share their dishes and recipes, expanding our culinary vocabulary. Our friends from Calcutta would speckle their dishes with mustard and sweeten with sugar. My Gujarati "aunties" loved using *methi*, the bitter leaves of the fenugreek plant, in just about everything. Our friends in the north taught us the ins and outs of the perfect, juicy chargrilled kebab.

Though the dishes and flavours vary geographically, one thing is a constant: spices. Spices are the holy grail of Indian cuisine. Cumin, coriander, turmeric, cinnamon, fennel seed, asafoetida, ajwain, and countless others all make Indian food so glorious. I'm often asked how one learns to put these spices together, and my best answer is *experimentation*. I've seen recipes that call for upward of twenty different spices in different proportions; the possibilities are indeed endless, but that shouldn't really intimidate you. Think of each spice as a colour that is just about to touch canvas. While it's nice to use measuring spoons and follow recipes word for word, I prefer to free-style with spices and encourage you to do the same. Note that large grocery stores carry a lot more spices than they ever did before. Learn which flavours you like together, and soon enough you'll be creating spice blends unique to your tastes. Use all your senses to make these recipes come alive. Always taste what you're making, hear the crackle of spices hitting hot oil, bask in the aroma of bubbling curries, feel the plump and supple doughs under your hands.

(Note that my threshold for heat is nowhere close to that of my parents and relatives, who eat green chilies like they're potato chips! My recipes in this chapter do veer toward mild, but of course you can always add more heat if you like.)

Get ready to flip this page and delve into my world of Indian cookery. The recipes, from familiar mouth-watering classics to regional specialties, are designed to transport you to the motherland. I hope that along the way you'll discover new cooking techniques, and flavour profiles that will have your taste buds doing their best Indian dance moves!

Anbudan,
Vijaya

Recipes

POORI

Serves 6 (makes about 20 poori)

Deep-fried breads that magically puff up into pillows or clouds. Excellent to snack on, or for serving at the dinner table.

4 cups (1 L) (500 g) all-purpose flour (plus extra for dusting)
1 Tbsp (15 mL) melted ghee (page 145)
Vegetable oil for deep-frying, about 4 cups (1 L)

Put the flour, ghee, and a pinch of salt in a large bowl, and mix in enough water to make a pliable dough. Knead for about 5 minutes in the bowl. Form into 2-inch (5 cm) balls. Using a rolling pin, roll out each ball on a lightly floured surface into a 5- to 6-inch-diameter (12–15 cm) round.

Line a baking sheet or large plate with paper towels. Heat the oil in a deep, heavy-bottomed pot or wok to 350°F (177°C) over medium-high heat.

Working in batches, carefully add the poori to the hot oil. Deep-fry for 1 to 2 minutes, or until puffed up and golden brown. Use a spoon to baste some of the oil onto the top side, and turn over once during the deep-fry. Remove the poori with a slotted spoon or spider, and drain on the paper towels.

Repeat with remaining dough. Serve hot.

GHEE
Makes 1¼ cups (310 mL)

Or as we like to call it: "butter of the gods." Make extra and slather it on a nice slice of rustic bread for a true taste awakening.

1 lb (450 g) butter (2 sticks)

Melt the butter in medium saucepan over medium-high heat. Bring to a simmer, which will take about 2 to 3 minutes, and then reduce the heat to medium. Skim off and discard the excess foam at the top. As the butter cooks, there will be less and less of this foam, and caramelized brown bits will start to cling to the bottom of the pan.

The ghee is done when another light-coloured foam forms on top of the butter, and the butter turns golden, 7 to 8 minutes from when it started simmering. Gently pour the ghee into a heatproof container (with an airtight lid) through a fine-mesh sieve or through cheesecloth.

Store in the refrigerator. It will keep for long time.

CHAPATI

Makes 20 chapati

This flatbread is super easy to make, and it keeps nicely for a while, so make extra when you're tired of pita or other wraps. It has a wonderful chew that holds up well to dipping into sauces, soups, and curries. You might also know it as *roti*.

3⅓ cups (415 g) whole wheat flour, plus extra for dusting

Pinch of salt

1 cup (250 mL) water

Melted ghee (page 145) or butter, for brushing (optional)

Sift the flour and salt into a large stainless-steel bowl. There may be a bit of bran left behind, which can be discarded.

Add the 1 cup (250 mL) water to the flour, and start mixing with your hands until a soft dough is formed. Knead in the bowl for 4 minutes. Cover and let rest for 30 minutes.

Divide the dough into 20 equal pieces, and form each into balls. Lightly dust the work surface with flour. Take one ball, and flatten between the palms of your hands and dust with flour. Using a rolling pin, roll out to a round that's about 5 inches (12 cm) in diameter and quite thin.

Preheat a heavy skillet (or flat tawa) over high heat, then reduce the heat to medium to medium-low. Add one chapati to the pan, and cook for about 10 seconds, when it should begin to bubble and puff up. Turn over the chapati and cook the other side.

The chapati is cooked when it completely puffs up and brown patches appear on the bottom surface. The dough will become lighter in colour.

Serve the chapati as they are, or brushed with ghee (or butter).

CHANA MASALA
Serves 6

This one comes from northern India, and is best described as tangy. It's actually a popular snack food sold on the streets in Pakistan. It features the ever-versatile chickpea (also known as chana or garbanzo bean), which really should be eaten more often. It's a great side dish alternative when you want to dress up Tuesday night dinner.

2 cans (each 14 oz/398 mL) chickpeas

2 to 3 Tbsp (30–45 mL) vegetable oil

1 Tbsp (15 mL) cumin seeds

1 onion, finely diced

2 tsp (10 mL) finely chopped garlic

2 tsp (10 mL) finely chopped fresh ginger

1 tsp (5 mL) chopped green serrano chilies (seeds removed)

1 Tbsp (15 mL) ground coriander

1 tsp (5 mL) garam masala (page 150)

1 tsp (5 mL) red chili powder

1 tsp (5 mL) ground turmeric

1 tsp (5 mL) kosher salt

1 can (28 oz/796 mL) diced tomatoes with their juice, or 3 chopped tomatoes

2 cups (500 mL) fresh spinach leaves (optional)

GARNISHES

½ red onion, thinly sliced

½ cup (125 mL) packed fresh cilantro leaves

½ cup (125 mL) plain yogurt (not low-fat) or sour cream

1 recipe poori (page 142)

Salt to taste

Drain the chickpeas and rinse well under cold water.

In a large skillet, heat the oil over medium heat until shimmering. Add the cumin and cook, stirring occasionally, until fragrant and slightly toasty, being careful not to burn (or the cumin will take on a bitter and off flavour).

Once toasted and fragrant, add the onion, garlic, ginger, and chilies. Increase the heat to medium-high, and cook until softened but not brown, about 5 minutes.

Add the coriander, garam masala, chili powder, turmeric, and salt, stirring to mix well. Add the tomatoes and their juices, the chickpeas, and a splash of water. Simmer for 20 to 30 minutes, or until the flavours are melded and the sauce is slightly thickened. Season with salt to taste. Fold in the spinach, if using.

If desired, serve with the red onion, cilantro, and yogurt (or sour cream), and/or freshly made poori.

...CONTINUED

GARAM MASALA
Makes about ¾ cup (185 mL)

The ratio of spices, and the spices themselves, varies from region to region—and household to household—much like a family's secret recipe for pasta sauce. Start from here, and then fiddle with the recipe as you become more familiar with what you like. I sometimes add four star anise to the recipe below. Make small batches at a time; spices are better when ground at the last minute, and you probably have an old coffee grinder in the basement.

3 Tbsp (45 mL) coriander seeds

3 Tbsp (45 mL) cumin seeds

2 tsp (10 mL) green cardamom pods

2 tsp (10 mL) black peppercorns

1 tsp (5 mL) cloves

Two 2-inch (5 cm) cinnamon sticks

4 bay leaves

Place a medium cast iron skillet over medium heat. Add all the ingredients, and toast, stirring constantly using a wooden spoon, until the seeds become fragrant, about 4 to 5 minutes. Make sure none of the spices burn, or the garam masala will become bitter.

Immediately transfer the spices from the skillet to a small bowl, and allow to cool. Transfer the spices to a spice grinder (or coffee grinder set aside for spices), and process until it becomes a fine powder.

INDIA

ONION PAKORA

Serves 6 as an appetizer

These tasty, deep-fried treats are classic Indian street food. Light, crunchy, and easy to make, they're perfect with our sweet cooling mint and cilantro chutney (see recipe on page 154) or even plain sour cream. We've also served these as an interesting appetizer at a chic dinner party where the rest of the meal was decidedly not Indian. We are One World Kitchen, and we believe in mixing things up.

1 cup plus 2 Tbsp (280 mL) chickpea flour (also sold as gram flour or besan)

1½ tsp (7.5 mL) baking powder

3 medium onions, thinly sliced

2 long green serrano or bird's eye chilies, seeds removed, finely chopped

¼ cup (60 mL) freshly chopped cilantro leaves

¾ cup (185 mL) water

1½ tsp (7.5 mL) kosher salt

Vegetable oil for deep-frying, about 4 cups (1 L)

Mint and cilantro chutney (page 154)

In a large bowl, combine the chickpea flour with the baking powder and mix well. Drop in the onions, chilies, and cilantro. Coat the vegetables with the flour mix, then slowly add the water. It should be like a thick pancake batter. If needed, add water a teaspoon (5 mL) at a time to make a stiff batter.

In a large heavy-bottomed pot or wok, heat enough oil to 350°F (177°C) over medium-high heat. Line a baking sheet with paper towels.

Working in batches and being careful not to overcrowd the pot (which would reduce the temperature of the oil), drop spoonfuls of the batter into the hot oil. Deep-fry, turning frequently, for 2 to 3 minutes, or until the pakoras are crispy, slightly puffed, and golden brown. Remove with a slotted spoon or spider, and drain on the paper towels.

Serve with the chutney.

MINT AND CILANTRO CHUTNEY
Makes 1½ cups (375 mL)

The word *chutney* derives from ancient Sanskrit and means "lick." In Indian cuisine, a number of chutneys are offered at the table; there is a countless variety. Chutney is a special kind of condiment, which can provide more heat or more fruitiness, or smooth out the meal. It can even cool the palate, which this one does. For you cilantro-phobes, try making this with parsley instead. Serve with pakora or your favourite flatbread.

½ cup (125 mL) packed fresh mint leaves
½ cup (125 mL) packed fresh cilantro
1 green serrano or bird's eye chili,
    seeds removed, finely chopped
1½ tsp (7.5 mL) finely chopped fresh ginger
1 Tbsp (15 mL) fresh lemon juice
½ cup (125 mL) plain yogurt (not low-fat)
Salt to taste

In a mini food chopper, the small bowl of a food processor, or a blender, process all of the ingredients. Pour into a serving bowl.

CROCK-POT DAL
Serves 6 to 8

For a while there, no one would be caught dead in the proximity of a slow cooker. Common sense now prevails, luckily, and the slow cooker is being brought up from basements everywhere. *Dal* is an Indian term for "dried pulses," which includes the whole family of peas, lentils, and beans. We recommend a combination here, but of course adjust the proportion to your tastes and to what you have or can find. Split mung beans are yellow and are also known as *moong dal*; split chickpeas (*chana dal*) are actually black chickpeas that have been polished and split.

3 cups (750 mL) mixed red lentils, yellow split peas, split mung beans, and split chickpeas
6 cups (1.5 L) water
2 tsp (10 mL) cumin seeds
2 tsp (10 mL) brown mustard seeds
2 tsp (10 mL) onion seeds (kalonji or nigella seeds)

2 tsp (10 mL) fenugreek seeds (methi seeds)
1 tsp (5 mL) fennel seeds
1 large Spanish onion, finely diced
4 cloves garlic, finely chopped
2 Tbsp (30 mL) freshly chopped ginger
3 green cardamom pods, crushed open
1 bay leaf

1 Tbsp (15 mL) ground turmeric
1 tsp (5 mL) kosher salt
¼ tsp (1 mL) freshly ground pepper
Fresh sprigs of cilantro, for garnish
Lemon wedges, for garnish
Store-bought papadums, to serve

Place the lentils, split peas, split mung beans, and split chickpeas into a large bowl, and cover with water. Let soak for a few minutes, then swish them around to rinse them, and drain well using a large sieve. Rinse more under cold water and drain again. Transfer to a slow cooker and add the water.

In a medium cast iron skillet, toast the seeds (cumin, mustard, onion, fenugreek, and fennel) over medium heat, shaking the pan or stirring constantly with a wooden spoon. When they start to smell fragrant, remove the skillet from the heat. Transfer the spices to the slow cooker.

Add the onions, garlic, ginger, cardamom, bay leaf, turmeric, salt, and pepper to the slow cooker, and stir well. Place the lid on the slow cooker, and cook on the low setting for 4 to 5 hours.

After the cooking time is up, give it a stir. If the dal isn't soft after 6 hours, cook for another 30 to 60 minutes. Season with more salt and freshly ground pepper, if needed.

Serve with cilantro and lemon wedges, and papadums on the side for dipping.

PEAS PULAO
Makes 8 cups (2 L)

A classic Indian side dish that will quickly become part of your go-to repertoire. Make extra—it rocks for lunch the next day, even served cold. It takes just a few more steps than regular old rice and is *so* worth the flavour boost.

1½ cups (375 mL) basmati rice (uncooked)

3 Tbsp (45 mL) ghee (page 145) or vegetable oil

1 tsp (5 mL) cumin seeds

1-inch (2.5 cm) piece cinnamon stick

2 cardamom pods, cracked open

2 cloves

1 bay leaf

½ cup (125 mL) thinly sliced onions (¼-inch/ 6 mm slices)

2¼ cups (560 mL) water, for cooking the rice

3 cups (750 mL) frozen sweet peas, quickly rinsed

Wash the basmati rice to remove the outer starch on the grain by swishing around the rice in a large bowl of water. Strain and repeat until the water runs clear. Place the strained rice in the bowl, cover again with water, and let soak for 30 minutes. Strain.

In a large heavy-bottomed pot that has a tight-fitting lid, melt the ghee (or heat the oil) over medium heat. Add the cumin seeds and let crackle and pop until fragrant (but don't let it burn). Add the cinnamon, cardamom, cloves, and bay leaf and toast until aromatic.

Add the onions and cook until soft and golden brown. Add the rice and stir gently into the onions.

Add the water, and season with salt. Cover tightly and cook for 15 minutes or until rice is cooked and the water is absorbed. Fluff with a fork and add the peas. Cover for 3 to 5 minutes. Fluff again.

Lemon Rice

RICE TWO WAYS: LEMON RICE AND COCONUT RICE

Serves 4 to 6

In the south of India, people just can't get enough of rice. Here are two recipes that add flavour to basmati after it's been cooked.

LEMON RICE

Juice 1 lemon

½ tsp (2.5 mL) ground
   turmeric

1 tsp (5 mL) kosher salt

2 Tbsp (30 mL) vegetable oil

3 dried red chilies

3 cups (750 mL) freshly
   cooked basmati rice
   (page 162)

½ cup (125 mL) freshly
   chopped cilantro

½ cup (125 mL) roasted
   cashews (see below)

COCONUT RICE

2 Tbsp (30 mL) vegetable oil

3 dried red chilies

½ cup (125 mL) dried
   unsweetened
   coconut flakes

3 cups (750 mL) freshly
   cooked basmati rice
   (page 162)

½ cup (125 mL) roasted
   cashews (see below),
   roughly chopped

½ cup (125 mL) roughly
   chopped fresh
   cilantro leaves

Toasted unsweetened
   coconut flakes, for garnish
   (optional)

LEMON RICE: In a small bowl, mix the lemon juice, turmeric, and salt. Stir to dissolve the salt, and then set aside.

Pour the oil into a medium skillet over medium heat. Add the chilies, and toast until blistered and aromatic. Remove from the pan and set aside.

Place the warm rice in a large bowl. Add the lemon juice mixture and toss to coat. Use your hands to break up the chilies and crumble them into the bowl. Gently fold in the cilantro and cashews.

COCONUT RICE Preheat a cast iron skillet over medium-low heat. Add the oil and heat for 1 minute. Add the dried chilies; once they start to blister and crackle on one side, turn over and cook the other side. When the chilies are fragrant, lightly browned, and crispy, remove them from the pan.

To the skillet add the coconut, stirring constantly until it's a light golden colour, about 45 seconds, being careful not to burn. Add the cooked rice, stirring to incorporate. Use your hands to break apart the toasted chilies, and mix them in. Gently fold in the cashews and cilantro, and season to taste with salt and freshly ground pepper.

Garnish with toasted coconut, if using.

HOW TO ROAST CASHEWS
Preheat a cast iron skillet over medium heat. Add the cashews and stir or shake the pan occasionally until they begin to turn golden brown. Be careful not to burn the cashews.

. . . CONTINUED

INDIA

BASMATI RICE

Makes 3 cups (750 mL) (serves 4 to 6)

Basmati really is a notch or two above regular and run-of-the-mill white rice. When rice is left soaking in water, the grains gently expand. Perfect rice is soft and fluffy with each grain separate, and will absorb the sauce and flavours of your main dish; it's worth it to perfect your technique.

1 cup (250 mL) good-quality basmati rice
2 cups (500 mL) water, for cooking the rice
Splash of melted ghee (page 145) or vegetable oil
1 tsp (5 mL) kosher salt

In a large sieve, rinse the rice under running water until the water runs clear; this will remove the outer starch of the grain. Place the rice in a bowl, cover with cold water, and let stand for at least 30 minutes. Drain the rice, and add it to a medium saucepan that has a tight-fitting lid.

Add the water and a splash of ghee (or oil), which will help the water from boiling over because of the starch in the rice.

Bring to a boil uncovered over medium-high heat. When it starts to boil, cover tightly, and reduce the heat to low. Cook for 15 minutes. Remove the lid and fluff with a fork.

INDIA

Coconut Rice

JEERA RICE
Serves 6

Jeera (cumin) perfumes the rice along with other spices you would typically find in a garam masala.

1½ cups (375 mL) basmati
  rice (uncooked)
2 Tbsp (30 mL) vegetable oil
2 tsp (10 mL) cumin
1-inch (2.5 cm) piece
  cinnamon stick
4 green cardamom
  pods, cracked open
1 bay leaf
2 to 3 cloves
5 to 6 black peppercorns
2 to 3 star anise
3 cups (750 mL) water
Fresh sprigs of cilantro,
  for garnish

Wash the basmati rice to remove the outer starch on the grain by swishing around the rice in a large bowl of water. Strain and repeat until the water runs clear. Place the rice in enough water to cover by 1 inch (2.5 cm), and soak for half an hour. Drain the rice and set it aside.

In a sauté pan or saucepan that has a tight-fitting lid, heat the oil over medium heat, then add the cumin and toast for 30 seconds. Add the rest of the spices (cinnamon, cardamom, bay leaf, cloves, peppercorns, and star anise), and stir and toast for 2 minutes, or until fragrant.

Stir in the rice. Add the 3 cups (750 mL) water and a pinch of salt, bring to a boil over medium-high heat, and cover tightly. Reduce the heat to low. Let the rice cook for 10 to 15 minutes, or until all of the water has been absorbed and rice is light and fluffy.

Using a fork, fluff the rice. Serve immediately, garnished with the cilantro sprigs.

CAULIFLOWER WITH ORANGES
Serves 6 to 8

We love this dish because it's so different from the common perception of Indian cuisine. Most people would never think of pairing cauliflower with oranges, yet the flavours (when boosted with garam maslala, ginger, and cumin) are a delight. Try this one out the next time you grill chicken.

1 small head cauliflower, about 2 lbs (1 kg), cut into 1-inch (2.5 cm) florets

2 potatoes, unpeeled, cut into 1-inch (2.5 cm) pieces

2 onions, cut into 1-inch (2.5 cm) pieces

1 tsp (5 mL) ground turmeric

¼ cup (60 mL) vegetable oil

2 tsp (10 mL) ground cumin

2 tsp (10 mL) garam masala (page 150)

1 tsp (5 mL) ground ginger

1 tsp (5 mL) red chili powder

3 oranges, peeled and divided into segments

1 tsp (5 mL) granulated sugar

½ cup (125 mL) water, or more if necessary

1 serrano or bird's eye chili, finely chopped (optional)

Place the cauliflower, onions, and potatoes in a large bowl, and sprinkle with the turmeric, tossing to coat.

Heat the oil in a large heavy-bottomed nonreactive skillet over high heat. Reduce the heat to medium, and add the vegetables. Stir-fry for 3 to 5 minutes, or until golden and lightly browned. Transfer the vegetables to a bowl, and set aside.

Add a touch more oil to the pan, still over medium heat. Add the cumin, garam masala, ground ginger, and chili powder, and roast until they begin to change colour and become increasingly fragrant.

Add the reserved vegetables to the pan, then add the oranges and sugar. Add the water to deglaze the pan. Cover and reduce the heat to a gentle simmer. Simmer for 15 minutes, or until the vegetables are cooked but are still slightly firm.

Add the chilies, if using, for the last 5 minutes of cooking time. Serve with rice.

MINT-MARINATED GRILLED SHRIMP

Serves 4 as a main course (makes 10 to 12 skewers)

The flecks of mint against the charred pink flesh of the shrimp creates a stunning presentation—*and* it's delicious. Ajwain seed—not exactly a seed, despite the name—has a bit of an oregano thing going on. We've put it in the recipe in case you're close to an Asian market, but this dish works just as well without it. Same goes for the curry leaves (which don't actually have anything to do with curry), and can easily be left out. Shrimp, on the other hand, are pretty essential. This would be a great main course with the Peas Pulao on page 158.

MARINADE

1½ tsp (7.5 mL) roughly chopped garlic

1 Spanish onion, coarsely chopped

2 cups (500 mL) loosely packed fresh mint leaves

2 cups (500 mL) loosely packed fresh cilantro leaves

2 fresh or dried curry leaves

3 Tbsp (45 mL) chopped green serrano or bird's eye chili

1¼ cups (310 mL) plain yogurt (not low-fat)

1 Tbsp (15 mL) chickpea flour (also sold as gram flour or besan)

1 tsp (5 mL) crushed black peppercorns

1 tsp (5 mL) ground cinnamon

1 tsp (5 mL) ajwain seeds

Pinch of ground allspice

1½ tsp (7.5 mL) finely chopped fresh ginger

4 tsp (20 mL) fresh lemon juice

FOR THE SHRIMP

2¼ lbs (1 kg) shrimp (21/25 count), peeled and deveined

2 Tbsp (30 mL) vegetable oil

Melted ghee (page 145), for final basting

EQUIPMENT

15 bamboo skewers, soaked in cold water for 15 minutes

Pound the garlic in a mortar and pestle to make a paste, and set aside. Place the onions, mint, cilantro, curry leaves, chilies, and yogurt into a blender and process until smooth. Transfer the mixture to a bowl, and add the reserved garlic paste and the rest of the marinade ingredients (chickpea flour, black pepper, cinnamon, ajwain, allspice, ginger, and lemon juice).

Place the shrimp in a shallow dish, and coat in the marinade. Cover with plastic wrap, and leave to marinate in the fridge for 30 minutes.

Preheat the grill to medium-high heat. Have read a wire rack placed on top of plate or baking sheet.

Remove the shrimp from the marinade, brushing off the excess. Thread 2 to 3 shrimp on skewers. Drizzle with the vegetable oil and season with salt and freshly ground pepper.

Place the shrimp on the grill, sliding a piece of aluminum foil under the exposed part of the skewers to prevent burning. Turn over after 2 minutes, and cook until shrimp is tender and pink.

Transfer the shrimp to a wire rack to let the excess moisture drip off. Brush the shrimp with ghee and place back on the grill for 1 more minute for final char marks.

FISH SIMMERED IN RED CHILI COCONUT CHUTNEY

Serves 4

Most of us think of curries and braises when we think of Indian cuisine. But remember, India is a large country surrounded by water on three sides; that means lots of fish, which is best served steamed, fried, or grilled. The marinade is simple, too, and you'll love how well these flavours complement the sweet, firm halibut. And there are only three ingredients in the chutney, but they create a contrasting flavour profile.

1 tsp (5 mL) ground turmeric

½ tsp (2.5 mL) granulated sugar

4 cloves garlic, crushed

1 Tbsp (15 mL) fresh lime juice

1½ lbs skinless fillets of firm white fish (such as halibut), divided into 4 equal portions

5 dried red chilies

⅓ cup dried unsweetened coconut flakes

1 tsp (5 mL) vinegar

1 Tbsp (15 mL) vegetable oil

½ cup (125 mL) water

Make a marinade by mixing together the turmeric, sugar, garlic, and lime juice in a bowl. Season with a pinch of salt and freshly ground pepper.

Place the fish in a large shallow dish, and coat with the marinade, rubbing it into the fish. Keep covered in the fridge, and marinate for no more than half an hour.

Place the chilies, coconut, vinegar, and a generous splash of water into a coffee grinder set aside for spices, mini food chopper, or the mini-bowl attachment of a food processor, and process to make a paste. If the mixture is too thick, add another splash of water. (You could also use a spice grinder to grind the chilies and coconut before mixing them with the vinegar and water in a small bowl.)

Heat the oil in a cast iron skillet over high heat. Add the chili and coconut paste, and stir-fry for 30 to 60 seconds (do not brown). Reduce the heat to medium, and ½ cup (125 mL) water to make it saucy. Once it simmers, add the fish.

Let simmer until the fish is cooked, 6 to 8 minutes depending on the thickness of the fish, turning them over once during the cooking time. Pry back some of the fish in the centre of a fillet; it should just be losing its translucent colour, and be almost fully opaque yet still really glossy.

Transfer to serving plates, and serve with rice.

PALAK PANEER

Serves 4 to 6

This is a north Indian curry featuring homemade paneer and puréed spinach (*palak*). You never have to worry about trying to find paneer at the store, as homemade is so much better anyway—and one of the easiest cheeses to make. All it takes is some curdling and straining. Make it the day before starting the curry. If you prefer more spice, add 1 teaspoon (5 mL) of red chili flakes to the onions, and also ½ cup (125 mL) of chopped tomatoes for a slight variation.

1 lb (450 g) fresh spinach, washed well, stems removed

1 small red bird's eye chili, seeds removed, cut in medium dice

3 Tbsp (45 mL) extra-virgin olive oil, divided

1 tsp (5 mL) cumin seeds

1 tsp (5 mL) garam masala (page 150)

1 cup (250 mL) diced Spanish onion

1 tsp (5 mL) finely chopped garlic

1 tsp (5 mL) finely chopped fresh ginger

½ cup (125 mL) heavy cream

1 recipe paneer (page 174)

1 Tbsp (15 mL) fresh lemon juice, to finish

Bring a large pot of water to a boil over high heat, and have ready a large bowl of ice water. Blanch the spinach for 30 seconds to 1 minute, and then remove using tongs, a slotted spoon, or a spider. Immediately plunge in the ice water (this helps the spinach to retain its bright green colour).

Squeeze out the water from the spinach. Place in a food processor along with the chili. Blend until smooth, and set aside.

Heat 2 tablespoons (30 mL) of the olive oil to a large skillet over medium heat. Add the cumin, garam masala, and onion, and cook for 3 minutes, or until the onions are soft. Add the garlic and ginger, and sauté for 1 minute or until fragrant. Add the reserved spinach purée and the cream, and simmer for 2 to 3 minutes. Keep warm.

Cut the finished paneer into 1-inch (2.5 cm) cubes. Line a plate with paper towels.

Heat the remaining 1 tablespoon (15 mL) olive oil in a medium skillet over medium-high heat. Cook the paneer until golden, turning frequently to brown on all sides. Let drain on the paper towels.

Add the paneer to the spinach and cream mixture, tossing to coat. Add the lemon juice, and salt to taste.

PANEER

4 cups (1 L) fresh whole milk
1 Tbsp (15 mL) fresh lemon juice
1 Tbsp (15 mL) water
Muslin or cheesecloth

Line a medium-size sieve with muslin or several layers of cheesecloth, and set it over a large bowl. Pour the milk into a heavy-bottomed saucepan, and bring slowly to a simmer over medium heat, stirring occasionally.

Remove the pan from the heat, and immediately add the lemon juice, stirring vigorously until the milk starts to curdle (you'll see the milk separating into curds and whey). Carefully strain the entire mixture through the lined sieve.

Let the whey drain off, about 6 hours or overnight, at room temperature.

The curds left in the sieve are known as chenna. Knead lightly in the sieve by hand until it becomes smooth. (Hang on to the muslin or cheesecloth, as you'll be using it again.)

Wrap the cheese using the same muslin or cheesecloth, and shape it into a square or rectangle. Make sure the paneer is wrapped tightly before placing it on a plate and under a cutting board with a heavy weight on top. Leave to drain further, at room temperature for 4 hours, or overnight in the refrigerator.

Unwrap the paneer, and cut into desired shapes.

CHICKEN TIKKA MASALA

Serves 6

Once you make this popular take-out dish yourself, your days of dial-and-dine are done. Much like the mix of spices sold as "curry powder," garam masala blends vary from region to region; however, peppercorns, cloves, nutmeg, and cardamom are the ingredients that most often show up. While garam masala is available in most big grocery stores, try making your own; spices are better when ground at the last minute. Give it a shot—you probably have an old coffee grinder in the basement!

YOGURT MARINADE

1 cup (250 mL) plain yogurt
   (not low-fat)
2 cloves garlic,
   finely chopped
1 Tbsp (15 mL) finely
   grated fresh ginger
1½ tsp (7.5 mL) ground cumin
1½ tsp (7.5 mL) ground
   coriander
¼ tsp (1 mL) ground
   cardamom
¼ tsp (1 mL) ground turmeric
Pinch of salt

FOR THE CHICKEN

2½ lbs (1.2 kg) skinless,
   boneless chicken breasts
4 Tbsp (60 mL) vegetable oil
   or melted ghee (page 145),
   divided
1 large onion, cut into ¼-inch
   (6 mm) slices
2 cloves garlic,
   finely chopped
1-inch (2.5 cm) piece
   fresh ginger, peeled
   and finely chopped
2 tsp (10 mL) garam masala
   (page 150)

1 tsp (5 mL) red chili powder
1½ cups (375 mL) canned
   diced tomatoes
½ cup (125 mL) water
1 tsp (5 mL) granulated sugar
1 cup (250 mL) full-fat
   sour cream
1 Tbsp (15 mL) sliced
   almonds, lightly toasted,
   for garnish
Fresh cilantro leaves,
   for garnish
Lime wedges, to serve

. . . CONTINUED

INDIA

Prepare the marinade by combining all of the ingredients in a bowl and mixing well.

Wash the chicken breasts, and pat dry using paper towels. Using a sharp knife, make 2 to 3 shallow slashes in each chicken breast. Place the meat in a shallow dish (or resealable plastic bag), and pour the yogurt marinade overtop. Make sure that all of the meat is well coated in the marinade. Cover with plastic wrap (or seal the bag), and leave in the fridge to marinate overnight.

Preheat your grill to medium-high, then clean and oil the grill grates to prevent sticking.

Scrape the marinade off of the chicken, and transfer to a large plate. Season the meat with salt and freshly ground pepper, and drizzle with 2 tablespoons (30 mL) of the oil (or ghee) to prevent sticking.

Grill for 3 minutes per side just until you get good char marks. (The chicken will finish cooking in the curry.) Let cool for a few minutes, then cut into 2-inch (5 cm) pieces. Set aside.

Heat the remaining 2 tablespoons (30 mL) of oil (or ghee) in a large heavy-bottomed nonreactive skillet over medium heat until shimmering. Add the onions, garlic, and ginger, and partially cover. Cook, stirring occasionally, for 8 to 10 minutes, or until the onions are soft and golden brown.

Add the garam masala and chili powder, and continue to cook for another few minutes, stirring often to avoid any burning. Add the tomatoes, water, and sugar, and season with salt and freshly ground pepper. Cover and reduce the heat to medium-low, and simmer for 10 minutes or until slightly thickened. Add the grilled chicken and simmer, stirring occasionally, for 8 to 10 minutes or until the chicken is cooked through.

Stir in the sour cream. Serve topped with the almonds, cilantro, and lime wedges.

BUTTER CHICKEN

Serves 6

Ah, butter chicken—the go-to Indian dish for anyone who thinks Dijon mustard is too spicy. Butter chicken is sweet, mild, and creamy, and is as mellow a dish as you'll ever find within the Indian culinary repertoire. Still, it's complex and earthy, and the sweetness isn't cloying if you make it yourself. Play with the spices until you achieve a mix your family can call their own. Pay particular attention to how much garam masala and cumin you add as they will alter the flavour profile considerably. This dish calls for chicken thighs; we find them richer in flavour, but breasts will do just as well.

MARINADE

1 Tbsp (15 mL) roughly chopped garlic

1 Tbsp (15 mL) roughly chopped fresh ginger

2 cups (500 mL) plain yogurt (not low-fat)

2 Tbsp (30 mL) red chili powder

2 tsp (10 mL) garam masala (page 150)

1½ tsp (7.5 mL) cumin seeds

1 tsp (5 mL) ground coriander

½ tsp (2.5 mL) ground turmeric

About 2 Tbsp (30 mL) fresh lime juice

FOR THE CHICKEN

2¼ lbs (1 kg) skinless, boneless chicken thighs, cut into 1-inch (2.5 cm) pieces

2 Tbsp (30 mL) ghee (page 145)

½ cup (125 mL) chilled butter (1 stick), divided

1¼ cups (310 mL) puréed canned tomatoes

1 tsp (5 mL) red chili powder

1 Tbsp (15 mL) granulated sugar

2 tsp (10 mL) dried fenugreek leaves (kasuri methi), crushed, plus more for garnish

1 tsp (5 mL) garam masala (page 150)

3 Tbsp (45 mL) heavy cream, plus more for drizzling

Fresh sprigs of cilantro, for garnish

. . . CONTINUED

For the marinade, first pound the garlic and ginger in a mortar and pestle until you have a paste. Transfer the paste to a shallow dish, and then add the rest of the marinade ingredients—yogurt, chili powder, garam masala, cumin, coriander, turmeric, and lime juice.

Rinse and pat the chicken dry using paper towels. Season with salt, then toss with the marinade. Cover and keep refrigerated for at least 2 hours or overnight.

Melt the ghee in a large heavy-bottomed sauté pan over medium heat. Add the chicken with just a little of the marinade to the pan. Cook, stirring occasionally, for 15 to 20 minutes, until the chicken is cooked, golden brown, and slightly crispy on the edges. Remove the chicken from the pan and set aside. Do not wash the pan.

Melt 1 tablespoon (15 mL) of the butter in the same pan over medium heat. Add the puréed tomatoes, and use a wooden spoon to scrape up any of the brown bits left in the pan from the chicken. Cook for 5 minutes or so, or until most of the moisture from the tomatoes has evaporated.

Melt the remaining 7 tablespoons (110 mL) butter in the tomatoes, then add the chili powder and sugar. Cook, stirring, for 5 minutes. Add the fenugreek leaves and garam masala, and season with salt if necessary.

Just before serving, stir in the cream, and add the reserved chicken to the pan to heat it through, tossing to coat. Serve with a sprinkle of crumbled fenugreek leaves, a drizzle of cream, a garnish of cilantro sprigs, and a side of rice.

CHICKEN XACUTI
Serves 6

Stop! Do not turn the page! Yes, there are a lot of ingredients in this recipe, but it's not a difficult dish to make. And we promise it's worth the effort. Try it on a Saturday or Sunday afternoon when you've got a bit of time (c'mon, not *everything* can be made in twenty minutes). And, the aroma! It's rich and sweet and profound all at once. It's the mixture of garlic, ginger, and coconut that smells so good. You'll want to make extra to add it to BBQ sauces and soups.

SPICE PASTE
1 Tbsp (15 mL) roughly chopped fresh ginger
1 Tbsp (15 mL roughly chopped garlic
8 dried long red chilies
1 Tbsp (15 mL) poppy seeds
1 Tbsp (15 mL) coriander seeds
10 black peppercorns
1½ tsp (7.5 mL) cumin seeds
1½ tsp (7.5 mL) fenugreek seeds (methi seeds)
½ cup (125 mL) dried unsweetened coconut flakes

FOR THE CHICKEN
Ghee (page 145) or vegetable oil
1 medium Spanish onion, cut into ⅛-inch (3 mm) slices
1 tsp (5 mL) ground turmeric
½ tsp (2.5 mL) ground cardamom
½ tsp (2.5 mL) ground cinnamon
½ tsp (2.5 mL) ground cloves
8 to 10 pieces skin-on, bone-in chicken thighs
1 cup (250 mL) water
Juice of 2 lemons

Preheat the oven to 350°F (180°C).

Place the ginger and garlic in a mortar and pestle along with a splash of water and some salt and freshly ground pepper. Pound until you have a smooth paste. Set aside.

In a heavy cast iron skillet set over medium-low heat, toast the chilies, poppy seeds, coriander, peppercorns, cumin, and fenugreek, stirring with a wooden spoon until the spices become fragrant. Be careful that the spices don't burn, as they will take on a bitter, off flavour. Add the coconut, and toast for 30 to 60 seconds or until golden brown, again being careful not to burn. Let the mixture cool.

Using a spice grinder (or a coffee grinder set aside for spices), grind the spices and coconut to a powder. Transfer to a bowl, and mix in the reserved ginger and garlic paste. Set aside.

Heat the ghee in a large heavy-bottomed ovenproof skillet over medium heat. Add the onions, reduce the heat to low, and cook until soft, browned, and caramelized, 40 minutes. Add the spice paste, and cook for 2 to 3 minutes to release the oils from the spices. Add the turmeric, cardamom, cinnamon, and cloves and stir to combine, then stir in the water.

Season the chicken thighs with salt and freshly ground pepper. Add them to the pan, and toss to coat in the sauce. Bake, uncovered, for 35 to 40 minutes. (After 20 minutes, check that the sauce is still covering the chicken, adding small amounts of water as needed.)

Just before serving, add the lemon juice to the pan. Serve with rice.

HARIYALI CHICKEN KEBAB
Serves 4 to 6

These may be the best chicken kebabs we've ever eaten. The spinach, cilantro, and mint in the marinade (along with the spices, ginger, and garlic) flavours the chicken and then becomes deliciously charred once the kebabs hit the grill. The meat is tender and juicy while crisp on the outside. Marinate the bird for as long as you can—overnight is best.

MARINADE

½ cup (125 mL) chopped fresh spinach leaves (stems removed)

1 cup (250 mL) fresh cilantro leaves

1 cup (250 mL) fresh mint leaves

2 Tbsp (30 mL) vegetable oil

½-inch (4 cm) piece fresh ginger

6 to 8 cloves garlic, roughly chopped

3 to 4 green serrano or bird's eye chilies, seeds removed, roughly chopped

2 tsp (10 mL) ground coriander

1 tsp (5 mL) ground cloves

1½ tsp (7.5 mL) garam masala (page 150)

½ tsp (2.5 mL) red chili powder

¼ tsp (1 mL) ground turmeric

3 Tbsp (45 mL) plain yogurt (not low-fat)

FOR THE CHICKEN

14 oz (400 g) skinless, boneless chicken breast

2 Spanish onions, cut into 1-inch (2.5 cm) wedges

3 lemons, cut into wedges for the kebabs, plus 1 halved lemon for final juicing

2 Tbsp (30 mL) vegetable oil

EQUIPMENT

Bamboo skewers, soaked in cold water for 15 minutes

To a food processor, add the spinach, cilantro, mint, ginger, garlic, fresh chilies, ground coriander, ground cloves, garam masala, chili powder, turmeric and vegetable oil, and blend to a fine purée. Add the yogurt, and process until well combined.

Wash the chicken, pat dry with paper towels, and cut into 1-inch (2.5 cm) cubes. Place in a bowl. Add the paste and toss to coat well. Cover the chicken, and leave to marinate in the refrigerator for at least 30 minutes or overnight.

Wipe off the excess marinade from the chicken. Thread pieces of chicken, onion wedges, and lemon wedge onto each skewer in an alternating pattern. Place the skewers on

a baking sheet. Drizzle the kebabs with the oil and sprinkle with salt.

Preheat the grill to medium (350°F/180°C), then clean and oil the grill grates to prevent sticking.

Lay the skewers on the grill, sliding a piece of aluminum foil under the exposed part of the skewers to prevent burning. Grill for 4 to 5 minutes per side, or until slightly crispy and golden and fully cooked.

Transfer the skewers to a plate, and tent loosely with foil, letting it rest for 5 minutes. When ready to serve, drizzle with the juice of a lemon.

LAMB AND BEEF KEBABS
Serves 6

Spiced ground meat shaped onto skewers—not what you'd normally picture as a kebab. (In North America, what we are really thinking of are *shish kebabs*.) Cashews, which are ground into a paste, lend a nice mouthfeel.

¼ cup (60 mL) cashews

1½ tsp (7.5 mL) roughly chopped garlic

1½ tsp (7.5 mL) roughly chopped fresh ginger

1 lb (450 g) ground lamb

1 lb (450 g) ground beef

1½ Tbsp (22.5 mL) garam masala (page 150)

1 Tbsp (15 mL) red chili powder

2 Tbsp (30 mL) melted ghee (page 145) or butter, plus more for basting the kebabs

Fresh sprigs of cilantro, for garnish (optional)

Thinly sliced red or green long chilies, for garnish (optional)

EQUIPMENT

Bamboo skewers, soaked in cold water for 15 minutes

Place the cashews in a small saucepan. Cover with 1 inch (2.5 cm) of water, bring to a simmer over medium-high heat, then reduce the heat to a simmer and cook for 5 to 10 minutes or until soft.

Drain through a colander, and let cool. Transfer to a coffee grinder, mini food chopper, or the mini-bowl attachment of your food processor, along with the garlic and ginger, and grind to a smooth paste. Set aside.

Preheat the grill to medium heat. Clean and oil the grill grates to prevent sticking.

Place the lamb in one bowl and beef in another. In a small bowl, combine the cashew paste, garam masala, chili powder, and ghee. Add half of this mixture to the lamb and the other half to the beef. Season with salt.

Water your hands, then take some of the lamb or beef and press it around a skewer to form a sausage-like shape. Form 8 lamb kebabs and 8 beef kebabs in total, placing them on a large plate or baking sheet to take to the grill.

Have ready a small bowl with the melted ghee (or butter) and a basting brush. Lay the kebabs on the grill, and slide a piece of aluminum foil under the exposed part of the skewers to prevent burning. Grill each side for 4 minutes, or until cooked to desired doneness. Every 2 minutes, baste the kebabs with the ghee (or butter). During the last minute of cooking, a final brush with ghee will help make the outside crispy.

Transfer the kebabs to a large plate, and tent with aluminum foil, letting them rest for 2 to 5 minutes. Garnish with cilantro sprigs and chilies, if desired.

ROGAN JOSH
Serves 6

Oh, lamb. Delectable lamb. Tender, melt-in-your-mouth lamb. Can you tell we love lamb? Rogan Josh lamb is crispified in nutty ghee, then bathed and simmered in earthy, sweet, piquant spices. This would work with stewing beef too, but then again, why would you want to?

6 saffron threads

1 Tbsp (30 mL) roughly chopped garlic

1 Tbsp (30 mL) roughly chopped fresh ginger

2½ lbs (1.1 kg) lamb leg or shoulder, cut into 1-inch (2.5 cm) cubes

1 cup (250 mL) ghee (page 145) or vegetable oil

6 peppercorns

4 cloves

1-inch (2.5 cm) piece cinnamon stick

1 tsp (5 mL) ground fennel

1½ cups (375 mL) sliced Spanish onions

2 tsp (10 mL) garam masala (page 150)

1 tsp (5 mL) red chili powder

1 cup (250 mL) plain yogurt (not low-fat), whisked

1 tsp (5 mL) granulated sugar

Long green and red serrano or bird's eye chili, thinly sliced, for garnish

Fresh sprigs of cilantro, for garnish

Heat ½ cup (125 mL) of water until hot but not boiling, and pour into a small bowl or mug with the saffron and let steep. Place the ginger, garlic, and water in a blender, coffee grinder set aside for spices, or a large mortar and pestle, and process until you have a smooth paste. Set aside the saffron water and the ginger and garlic.

Season the lamb with salt and freshly ground pepper. Preheat a large heavy-bottomed pot over medium heat, then add the ghee (or oil). When melted and hot, add the lamb, and cook until seared and dark brown on all sides, in batches if necessary. Crispy bits will appear on the edges of the lamb. This should take about 15 to 20 minutes for each batch. Set aside. Do not empty the pot of the ghee.

Place the pot over low heat. Cook the peppercorns, cloves, cinnamon stick, and fennel until fragrant. Add the onions and the ginger and garlic paste, and simmer, stirring often (to avoid burning), for 5 to 10 minutes or until reddish sediment begins to appear.

Add the garam masala and chili powder, and cook for 2 minutes. Add the yogurt, sugar, and the reserved saffron water. Simmer for 30 to 40 minutes, or until the meat is tender and there is very little sauce left. Add water if necessary.

Garnish with chilies and cilantro, and serve with rice.

LAMB CHOPS WITH CHILI AND TAMARIND
Serves 2 to 3

Tamarind paste—readily available in most grocery stores—comes from the fruit of the tamarind tree. Its sour, tart taste is essential to the balancing of flavours in Indian and other Asian cuisines. A little jar lasts for ages in the fridge. Again, marinating is important as it allows the spice mixture to perfume the lamb chops.

8 lamb chops cut from a Frenched rack of lamb or 8 lamb loin chops, 1 inch (2.5 cm) thick, trimmed of excess fat

COORGI MASALA MARINADE

2 Tbsp (30 mL) coriander

2 tsp (10 mL) fenugreek seeds

2 green cardamom pods

1 clove

1 bay leaf

½ star anise

1 Tbsp (15 mL) red chili powder

1½ tsp (7.5 mL) ground turmeric

1½ tsp (7.5 mL) roughly chopped garlic

1½ tsp (7.5 mL) roughly chopped fresh ginger

2 Tbsp (30 mL) white sesame seeds

1½ Tbsp (22.5 mL) fresh lemon juice

1 tsp (5 mL) Indian tamarind concentrate (also sold as "tamarind paste")

Place the chops in a large shallow dish.

Combine the first 6 coorgi masala spices—coriander, fenugreek, cardamom, clove, bay leaf, and star anise—into a spice grinder (or coffee grinder set aside for spices), and grind into a powder. Transfer the powder to a bowl, and add the chili powder and turmeric. Pound the garlic and ginger in a mortar and pestle until you have a smooth paste. Add to the spices along with the sesame seeds, lemon juice, tamarind, plus a pinch of salt, and stir to combine.

Rub the marinade over the chops until well coated. Cover and leave in the fridge to marinate for 30 minutes or overnight.

Let the lamb come to room temperature before grilling. Preheat the grill to medium-high, then clean and oil the grill grates to prevent sticking.

If you're using Frenched lamb chops, wrap the bones of the lamb in aluminum foil to prevent burning. Drizzle the lamb with oil, and sprinkle with salt and freshly ground pepper. Grill the lamb for 3 minutes per side or until desired doneness. Remove from the grill, and tent with foil for a few minutes before serving.

YOGURT LAMB CHOPS

Serves 2 (4 lamb chops per person)

The tanginess of yogurt and lemon juice, combined with fragrant spices, makes these lamb chops an exceptional addition to your BBQ repertoire. Spicy garam masala, earthy cumin, and sweet nutmeg works beautifully with the natural flavour of the lamb.

MARINADE

2 tsp (10 mL) roughly
chopped garlic

2 tsp (10 mL) roughly
chopped fresh ginger

¾ cup (185 mL) plain yogurt
(not low-fat)

3 Tbsp (45 mL) fresh
lemon juice

1 Tbsp (15 mL) garam masala
(page 150)

1 Tbsp (15 mL) ground cumin

¼ tsp (1 mL) freshly
grated nutmeg

FOR THE LAMB

8 lamb chops cut from a
Frenched rack of lamb or
8 lamb loin chops, 1 inch
(2.5 cm) thick, trimmed
of excess fat

2 Tbsp (30 mL) vegetable oil

Lemon wedges, to serve

Pound the garlic and ginger in a mortar and pestle until you have a smooth paste. Transfer to a small bowl, and mix in the rest of the marinade ingredients.

Place the lamb chops in a shallow dish, and coat the lamb with the marinade on all sides. Cover with plastic wrap, and leave in the refrigerator to marinate overnight.

Allow the lamb to come to room temperature before grilling. Brush off the excess marinade, drizzle with the oil on both sides to prevent sticking, and season with salt and freshly ground pepper.

Preheat the grill to medium-high, then clean and oil the grill grates to prevent sticking.

Grill the chops for 3 to 4 minutes per side for medium-rare. Transfer to a plate, and tent with aluminum foil for 3 to 5 minutes before serving.

Serve with lemon wedges.

ONION-TOMATO RAITA

Makes 1¼ cups (310 mL)

Raita should be the Indian word for "versatile" because this simple yogurt dish can be a sauce, dressing, or dip. Pretty sure that someone once said to themselves, "I wonder what I have in the fridge that I can mix with this leftover yogurt?" And so raita was invented. Our version combines crunchy onion with the sweet and tart taste of tomato. Adjust the heat level as you wish.

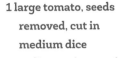

1 large tomato, seeds
    removed, cut in
    medium dice
1 medium onion, cut into
    ⅛-inch (3 mm) slices
1 green serrano or bird's eye
    chili, seeds removed,
    finely chopped
1 cup (250 mL) plain yogurt
    (not low-fat)
¼ cup (60 mL) fresh mint
    leaves, loosely torn
½ tsp (2.5 mL) toasted
    ground cumin
Fine Himalayan black
    salt (kala nanak),
    to taste (optional)
Fresh cilantro leaves
    (optional)

In a medium bowl, combine the tomatoes, onions, chilies, and yogurt. Add the mint and cumin, and the black salt to taste. Stir to combine.

CUCUMBER RAITA

Makes 3 cups (750 mL)

Another version of raita, the palate-cleansing side dish. For cilantro haters, consider substituting parsley and/or chives.

2 English cucumbers or
  6 Lebanese cucumbers
1 tsp (5 mL) ground cumin
¼ tsp (1 mL) kosher salt
2 cups (500 mL) plain yogurt
  (not low-fat)
½ cup (125 mL) freshly
  chopped cilantro

Peel, seed, and grate the cucumbers with a box grater. Place the cucumber in a tea towel, and squeeze out the moisture from the cucumber, discarding the liquid. Place in bowl.

Season with cumin and salt, then add the yogurt and stir to combine. Taste and adjust the seasonings. Cover and keep refrigerated until ready to serve.

Add the cilantro just before serving.

MANGO CHUTNEY

Makes 1½ cups (375 mL)

A sweet chutney to complement spicy Indian curries, but particularly lovely with grilled fish. The advantage to making this chutney yourself is that you can adjust the amount of sweetness and heat. Jaggery is an unrefined sugar, varying from golden to dark brown, usually made from the sap of palm trees but also from sugar cane. It has a buttery caramel- and molasses-like flavour. They're usually sold in blocks, and readily available at the Indian grocery store.

2 ripe mangoes, peeled and cut into ¼-inch (6 mm) dice
Juice of 1 lime
1 cup (250 ml) dried unsweetened coconut flakes
1 to 2 red bird's eye chilies
Grated jaggery, brown sugar, or palm sugar, to taste
½ cup (125 mL) freshly chopped cilantro leaves (optional)

In a bowl, combine the mangoes, lime juice, coconut, and chilies. Season with jaggery (or brown sugar or palm sugar) and salt to taste. Add cilantro, if using. Mix and serve.

MANGO PICKLES
Makes 5 to 6 cups (1.25–1.5 L)

Tired of the same old dill pickle? The secret here is to use green mangoes, whose flesh holds up to the pickling process and whose sweetness doesn't dominate. Any hard and unripe mango will work here. Asafoetida (or *hing*) is a powder derived from a tree resin, and while it may not smell very good, once it's cooked (or pickled, in this case), it becomes a gorgeously smooth, savoury flavour. Mustard oil adds a sharp and intense flavour just right for these pickles.

5 to 6 green mangoes

1 Tbsp (15 mL) ground turmeric

3 to 4 Tbsp (45–60 mL) kosher salt

1½ Tbsp (22.5 mL) red chili powder

1½ Tbsp (22.5 mL) brown mustard seeds

1½ Tbsp (22.5 mL) fenugreek seeds (methi seeds)

1 Tbsp (15 mL) asafoetida (hing)

2 Tbsp (30 mL) grated jaggery (see the headnote on page 201), brown sugar, or palm sugar

1½ to 2 cups (375–500 mL) mustard oil or vegetable oil

EQUIPMENT
Several glass jars with lids

Line a baking sheet with parchment paper.

Peel and cut the mangoes into ½-inch (1 cm) dice. Mix the turmeric and salt together, and coat the mangoes with the mixture, laying them out on the parchment-lined baking sheet. Cover loosely with plastic wrap and lay out on the counter overnight to dry out.

The next day, in a medium bowl, combine the chili powder, mustard seed, fenugreek, asafoetida, and the jaggery (or brown sugar or palm sugar). Add the mangoes, and coat evenly with the spices.

Transfer to the Mason jars, and pour in the mustard oil (or vegetable oil) until the mangoes are covered by 1 inch (2.5 cm). Cover the top of the jars with a tea towel or muslin to keep the dust out, and store in a cool and dry place for 3 to 4 days. Then replace the lid of the jar. Keeps for several weeks in the fridge.

PINEAPPLE KESARI

Serves 6 to 8

Want to try something different for dessert? Think of this as pineapple pudding, Indian style. The recipe is *so* easy, compared to, say, making a cheesecake. The combination of raisins, pineapple, and cashews with the ghee and cardamom will wow your dinner guests.

1½ cups (375 mL) milk

1 tsp (5 mL) saffron, about 6 to 8 threads

4 Tbsp (60 mL) ghee (page 145) or vegetable oil, divided

12 cashews

12 golden raisins

¼ tsp (1 mL) ground cardamom

1 cup (250 mL) semolina flour (rava)

1 cup (250 mL) canned crushed pineapple, drained but reserving ¾ cup (185 mL) of the juice

1 cup (250 mL) granulated sugar

Heat milk in a small saucepan over low heat. Remove the pan from the heat, add the saffron threads, and steep for 10 minutes.

Strain the saffron milk into a medium saucepan. Bring to a gentle simmer over medium-low. Remove the pan from the heat and set aside.

In a skillet set over medium-low, heat 2 tablespoons (30 mL) of the ghee (or vegetable oil). Add the cashews, raisins, and cardamom, and gently toast for 2 to 3 minutes. Remove the cashews and raisins from the pan and set aside.

To the same pan, add the remaining 2 tablespoons (30 mL) ghee (or vegetable oil) and heat over medium-low. Add the semolina and cook, stirring often with a wooden spoon to avoid burning, for about 2 minutes or just lightly toasted. Set aside.

Add the pineapple and pineapple juice to the milk, bring to a simmer, and allow to simmer over medium heat for a few minutes. Add the semolina to the milk, and whisk to combine. Simmer for 6 to 10 minutes, stirring occasionally. Add the sugar, and continue to simmer, stirring, for another 5 minutes. Fold in the cashews and raisins. (Alternately, instead of folding them in, you can serve the kesari with the cashews and raisins on top.)

Remove the pan from the heat. Serve the kesari immediately, or chill it to enjoy cold.

COCONUT BARFI

Makes one 8-inch or 9-inch (20-23 cm) square or round pan or thali

Okay, so over here in North America, the word "barfi" might have you thinking of something else, but these sweet, fudge-like squares are *addictive*. The coconut is perfectly offset by the sweet cardamom, rich condensed milk, and nutty ghee. Put a plate of these out on the counter and see how long they last.

3 to 4 green cardamom pods

¾ cup (185 mL) whole milk

1 cup (250 mL) dried
    unsweetened
    coconut flakes

2 tsp (10 mL) ghee
    (page 145)

¾ cup (185 mL) sweetened
    condensed milk

½ tsp (2.5 mL) rosewater
    (optional)

½ cup (125 mL) chopped
    pistachios

Butter an 8-inch or 9-inch (20 or 23 cm) round or square cake pan or thali (flat metal plate).

Grind the cardamom in a spice grinder (or a coffee grinder set aside for spices) until it's a powder. Or empty the seeds from the pods by crushing them open in a mortar and pestle, then pound the seeds into a powder. Set aside.

Warm the whole milk in a medium saucepan over medium heat. Remove the pan from the heat, and add the dried coconut, mixing to incorporate. Cover the saucepan and allow to soak for 1 hour.

Melt the ghee in a medium saucepan over low heat, and then add the soaked coconut (or fresh coconut). Toast for 2 to 3 minutes. Add the whole milk, condensed milk and the reserved cardamom, and cook, stirring constantly (to make sure it doesn't burn), until the mixture slowly thickens, 20 to 25 minutes.

At this point, you should see tiny drops of ghee forming on the surface of the mixture. Add the rosewater, if using, and remove the pan from heat.

Pour the mixture into the prepared pan. Press in the pistachios on top, and allow to cool completely. Slice into desired shapes and serve.

Will keep refrigerated for 2 days.

GULAB JAMUN
Makes about 20 balls

This is one of our favourite Indian desserts. You can call them Indian doughnut holes, doused in rosewater sugar syrup. They are amazing served hot with pistachio ice cream or gelato.

1 cup (250 mL) powdered
    milk, plus more as needed
3 Tbsp (45 mL) all-purpose
    flour
½ tsp (2.5 mL) baking soda
¼ tsp (1 mL) ground
    cardamom, for the dough
2 Tbsp (30 mL) whole milk
1 cup (250 mL) water
1¼ cups (310 mL) granulated
    sugar
1 tsp (5 mL) rosewater
Pinch of cardamom,
    for the syrup
Vegetable oil for deep-frying,
    about 4 cups (1 L)
Chopped pistachios, for
    garnish (optional)
Good-quality pistachio ice
    cream or gelato, to serve
    (optional)

In a bowl, mix the powdered milk, flour, baking soda, and cardamom until well combined. Add the milk. Stir until it becomes a medium-soft dough; it should still be slightly firm. You may need to add more milk powder. Cover and leave to rest for 20 minutes.

Prepare the rosewater syrup. In a medium saucepan, place the water, sugar, rosewater, and cardamom over medium-high heat. Bring to a boil. Reduce the heat to a simmer, and cook for 3 to 5 minutes. Set aside.

Heat the oil to 375°F (191°C) in a deep heavy-bottomed pot or wok. Line a baking sheet or plate with paper towels.

Form the dough into ¾-inch (2 cm) balls; the dough will almost double in size when deep-fried. And make sure the balls don't have any cracks, as cracked dough will most likely break when they are soaked in the syrup. (If there are cracks, add a little milk to the dough.)

Deep-fry 4 to 5 balls at a time, turning often, for about 5 minutes. The balls will puff up, turn golden brown, and float when fully cooked. Using a slotted spoon or spider, remove the balls from the oil, and drain on the paper towels.

Allow them to cool slightly, then place the balls into the pot with the rosewater syrup. Let sit for 10 to 12 minutes so that the balls absorb the syrup and puff up some more. Remove from syrup and place on plate.

Serve hot or cold, with pistachios on top and a scoop of pistachio ice cream on the side, if desired.

MANGO LASSI

Serves 2

India's answer to the smoothie, but meant to be enjoyed alongside any spicy main meal. For a lighter drink, blend with 1 cup (250 mL) ice.

2 cups (500 mL) cubed ripe
   mango (3 to 4 mangoes),
   chilled
¼ cup (60 mL) honey
   (optional)
2 cups (500 mL) plain yogurt
   (not low-fat), chilled
½ tsp (2.5 mL) ground
   cardamom
Fresh sprigs of mint,
   for garnish

Place the mangoes into a blender, and add the honey, but decrease or omit if the mangoes are really ripe and sweet. Purée. Add the yogurt and cardamom and blend again until smooth. Garnish with a mint sprig.

JAPAN

Hana Etsuko Dethlefsen

There's a feeling I get when I eat Japanese food. My shoulders relax. My back sinks into my chair. After the first sip of miso soup, I can finally breathe out for what suddenly feels like the first time that day. It's hard to pin down this feeling—it's just . . . home.

I didn't grow up in Japan, but I did grow up eating my mom's Japanese food. Everywhere I was in Vancouver, from home to my parents' friends' houses to the corner restaurant on campus, there it was—Japanese food. In this city, people are well versed in the menus of Japanese restaurants, and Japanese food here is a part of our everyday world.

It took a move to Japan to realize just how special Vancouver is. In Japan, I met ex-pats from outside of the Pacific Rim, and I realized that not everyone had the same familiarity with Japanese food that I did. My fellow ex-pats didn't know much else about what real Japanese people ate apart from sushi. During my three years in Japan, I rediscovered Japanese food through the eyes of my ex-pat friends. Eating with them made me see what was strange, surprising, or even straight-up illogical from an outsider's point of view. I also discovered that I loved sharing my passion for Japanese food, and that I wanted to know more about my "home" cuisine.

And what better place than Japan to start a self-initiated, self-guided training course in Japanese cookery and cuisine. I ate and cooked my way to happiness. Colleagues introduced me to tiny specialized restaurants. There was the little soba noodle shop on the side of the highway. The hotpot restaurants where we'd eat and cook together, adding ingredients to the communal pot at the centre of the table. When feeling flush, I travelled into Kyoto or Osaka to eat fancy *kaiseki* meals—an array of tiny, thoughtfully and exquisitely presented dishes inspired by seasonal ingredients. On rainy Sundays, I took a train for an hour and a half to a small town in the south of Nara prefecture, where I'd visit my Japanese-American friend Nana. We spent the afternoon in the public baths, soaking outdoors in aromatic cedar tubs, and then would walk, still steaming, to the local udon noodle shop famous for their *sanuki*-style (firm) noodles. Alongside my bowl of udon noodle soup, I couldn't help but also order a bowl of rice topped with *ebifurai*—giant deep-fried breaded prawns smothered in tartar

sauce. Out in the countryside, my friend Masayo drove me past miles of tiered rice paddies. We parked and walked past a tethered goat into an old farmhouse. There I was astounded by course after course of vegetarian dishes, all made from organic produce grown on the property—all the way down to the rice dusted with dried, powdered shiso herb. I couldn't believe my luck. I was eating the best food I'd ever had in my life.

I tried to re-create dishes or use what I had learned to create my own. I spent hours in the grocery store, developing an intimate knowledge of every aisle. Here were the one-litre Tetra Paks of sake; there, the milk and the drinking yogurt (not to be mixed up). Every visit finished with a trip to the tofu section, for a one-serving size piece of jiggly, bouncy goma (sesame) tofu. And in between the weekly grocery store visits, I purchased vegetables from a glass vending machine by the train tracks. (Yes, it's a real thing . . .)

But what made me really "get it" were trips to my grandparents' home in the Kyoto prefecture. I would hop on the train and then be picked up by my grandfather, who'd drive me to the tiny village where my mother had grown up. I decided to cook for my grandparents, experimenting with the vegetables gifted to us by neighbours stopping in for tea. Each time I unfolded a newspaper-wrapped offering, I discovered my next culinary challenge. A crinkly, pale green and white napa cabbage? A cluster of narrow eggplants? A pile of sharply flavoured green shishito peppers? Whatever it happened to be, I loved cooking with the vegetables grown by the old, retired farmers, bent from their years in rice paddies. Whether or not the dishes turned out well, cooking those vegetables connected me to the history and culture of my family. It may sound a bit romantic, but it was all entirely practical. These vegetables kept people fed between visits from the grocery truck because there wasn't a grocery store in town.

It was this that made me understand that Japanese cooking is, at its core, simple. Yes, the culinary culture is complex. And yes, in Japan chefs can spend their entire lives specializing in a particular dish, and farmers can spend generations producing the perfect ingredient. But all of that complexity developed from exactly what I had experienced at my grandparents' home—taking whatever was fresh and available, and trying to make it taste as good as it can be. And that's what I want to share with people—that Japanese food is simple food, and that it's something every-one can do at home. People have all sorts of impressions about Japanese food, but one thing is for sure: you can make it at home. The most difficult part will probably be learning about a few new ingredients. The cooking itself? Easy.

Hava
花刈

Recipes

THOUSAND-SLICE TURNIP PICKLE

Makes a 1-quart (1 L) jar

Pickling is all the rage, but people rarely think of pickling turnip. They're sweet and crunchy and the perfect side to your next big sandwich or burger. It's also good with Japanese curry (page 267). Kombu is thick, dark-coloured kelp that is sold dried.

2 lbs (900 g) turnips
    (about 5 medium)
2 Tbsp (30 mL) kosher salt
1½ tsp (7.5 mL) finely
    chopped fresh ginger
1½ tsp (7.5 mL) red
    chili flakes
1 piece of kombu (dried kelp),
    3 inches (8 cm) square,
    torn into little pieces
    (or ¼ tsp/1 mL MSG/
    ajinomoto)

PICKLING LIQUID
¼ cup (60 mL) rice vinegar
½ tsp (2.5 mL) kosher salt
1 tsp (5 mL) granulated sugar
½ cup (125 mL) water

Sterilize a 1-quart (1 L) jar by boiling it in water in large stockpot.

If the turnips have blemishes, peel off the skin, but otherwise you can leave it on. Cut them in half lengthwise, then slice crosswise as thin as possible (1/16 inch/2 mm), using a mandoline or a very sharp chef's knife. Place in a big bowl, sprinkle with the salt, and massage it into the turnips well. Let stand for half an hour.

In the meantime, prepare the pickling liquid. In a small bowl, mix all the ingredients together until the sugar and salt have dissolved. Set aside.

Drain and squeeze the excess water from the turnips. In the sterilized jar, layer the turnip with a sprinkle of the ginger, chili flakes, and kombu. Repeat until all the turnip slices and the aromatics are packed tightly.

Pour in the pickling liquid. If it doesn't cover the turnips, just top it up with water just to cover. Close the lid of the jar and refrigerate for 3 to 4 days before eating.

Keeps well in the fridge for 3 weeks.

SMASHED CUCUMBER PICKLES WITH GARLIC

Serves 2 to 4

Tatari kyuri, literally "beaten cucumbers." Gently smashing the cucumber allows the pickling ingredients to infuse the flesh. Japanese cucumbers are thin and seedless; substitute seeded Lebanese cucumbers.

1¾ lbs (800 g)
  Japanese cucumbers
  (5 or 6 medium)
2 cloves garlic, roughly
  chopped
1½ Tbsp (22.5 mL)
  rice vinegar
2 tsp (10 mL) granulated
  sugar
2 tsp (10 mL) kosher salt
Shiso or chives for garnish

Lay the cucumbers on a large cutting board, and bang them gently but firmly with a Japanese pestle or rolling pin to slightly smash the cucumbers, which will form cracks in the surface. Break into rough chunks with your hands, and drop into a large resealable freezer bag.

Mash the garlic with a pinch of the salt. You can use a mortar and pestle, or mash the garlic with the side of a chef's knife, sprinkle with the salt, and chop finely.

Sprinkle the 2 teaspoons (10 mL) of salt over the cucumbers, add the garlic purée along with the rice vinegar and sugar, and massage lightly to distribute. Roll up the bag to squeeze out as much of the air as possible, then refrigerate for about 10 minutes.

When ready to eat, drain the cucumbers in a fine-mesh sieve set over a bowl. Serve with ice-cold beer.

SUNOMONO

Serves 4 to 6

Sweet, tart, and crisp, this cucumber salad is the perfect side dish even when the rest of your meal might not be Japanese. Wakame is a mild seaweed that you often find in Japanese salads and in miso soup. They are sold dried in most Asian markets.

3 Japanese or 4 Persian
   cucumbers
1 tsp (5 mL) kosher salt
3 Tbsp (45 mL) rice vinegar
1 Tbsp (15 mL) granulated
   sugar
1 tsp (5 mL) soy sauce
1 tsp (5 mL) sesame seeds
¼ cup (60 mL) wakame,
   soaked in hot water for
   10 minutes, drained

Slice the cucumbers as thinly, about ⅛ inch (3 mm) thick, using a mandoline or a sharp chef's knife. Transfer to a colander or large sieve over a bowl, and massage in the salt. Let it sit for 5 minutes.

In a small bowl, combine the rice vinegar, sugar, and soy sauce, and stir until the sugar dissolves.

Squeeze the cucumbers of its excess liquid, and transfer to a bowl. Also drain the wakame, and add to the cucumber. Add the dressing along with the sesame seeds and mix well.

DAIKON AND DAIKON LEAF SALAD

Serves 4

Daikon radish is available in most grocery stores. Long, thin, and white, it has a crunch you'd expect from a radish, but with a milder, tangy flavour. It's excellent grated, steamed, fried, chopped, sautéed . . . you get the idea. Here we make a salad from both the radish and its green leaves, flavouring it with a triple hit of tart from the lemon, Dijon, and rice vinegar. And it's all balanced out with the saltiness of miso paste and dashi stock.

1 medium-small daikon
    (about 1¼ lbs/570 g), with
    leaves if available
2 green onions, thinly sliced
¼ cup (60 mL) red miso paste
1 tsp (5 mL) Dijon mustard
¼ cup (60 mL) dashi stock
    (see below) or water
Juice and zest of 1 lemon
1 Tbsp (15 mL) rice vinegar
1 tsp (5 mL) finely
    chopped fresh ginger
¼ cup (60 mL) vegetable oil

Peel the daikon and slice into 2- by ¼-inch (5 cm × 6 mm) julienne. Place in a colander. Chop a large handful of the tenderest leaves, if using, and add to the daikon along with the green onions. Sprinkle with salt and massage it in gently. Let sit for 10 minutes in a colander to drain.

In a small bowl, muddle together the red miso, mustard, ginger, and dashi stock (or water). Add the lemon zest and juice and the vinegar. Whisk in the oil until emulsified.

Squeeze the daikon and daikon leaves in handfuls of excess liquid, and drop into a clean serving bowl. Toss with the dressing and serve.

DASHI STOCK
Use dashi stock powder (dashi no moto), which is made from bonito flakes, for instant dashi stock. Dissolve ½ teaspoon (2.5 mL) for every 1 cup (250 mL) of hot water.

WARM DAIKON WITH MISO SAUCE
Serves 6 as a side dish

Daikon, so crispy when raw, becomes comfort food when cooked. Kombu is a thick dark-green seaweed, sold dried, and because of its saltiness and umami, is a common component of Japanese stocks. Other items to pick up at the Japanese shop: daikon radish sprouts, which have some of the peppery bite of the vegetable; mirin, a rice wine that's sweeter than sake and used for cooking; and finally, yuzu, a very special citrus fruit slowly gaining in popularity in North America. This last item, however, will probably be hard to find, so just use lemon juice instead.

1 large daikon radish
    (about 2 lbs/900 g)
1 piece of kombu (dried kelp),
    3½ inches (9 cm) square
2 to 3 green onions, thinly
    sliced, for garnish
Daikon radish sprouts,
    for garnish (optional)
Splash of fresh lemon
    juice or yuzu juice
    (if you can find it)

DRESSING
⅔ cup (160 mL) miso paste
3 Tbsp (45 mL) sake
2 Tbsp (30 mL) mirin
    (Japanese cooking wine)
1 Tbsp (15 mL) granulated
    sugar, plus more as needed
Splash of dashi stock
    (see the tip on page 223),
    plus more as needed
1 large egg yolk

Peel the daikon and cut into ¾- to 1-inch (2 to 2.5 cm) rounds. If you don't have a flat lid that's slightly smaller than the diameter of your medium saucepan, cut out a circle using parchment paper, and cut out a small air vent. Place the daikon in the medium saucepan, and add the kombu and water to cover. Bring to a simmer over medium heat. Cover with the small flat lid or parchment paper directly on top of the daikon. Cook until the daikon becomes slightly translucent, about 30 minutes.

While the daikon cooks, make the dressing. Bring a medium saucepan filled with water to a boil, then reduce to just a simmer over medium-low. In a stainless-steel bowl that fits over the pot, soften the miso by gradually mixing in the sake and mirin. Add the sugar and a splash of dashi stock, and whisk in the egg yolk. Cook, whisking constantly, until slightly thick, about 2 minutes. Taste and add more sugar if needed. If the sauce becomes too thick, whisk in a little dashi stock.

Using a slotted spoon, transfer daikon pieces to individual plates. Drizzle with the dressing. Garnish with the green onions, and daikon sprouts, if using. Drizzle with a splash of lemon juice (or yuzu juice) just before serving.

FOIL-BAKED SHIMEJI MUSHROOMS

Serves 4 to 6

Shimeji, also know as beech mushrooms, is a popular mushroom in Japan; the Japanese grocery should carry them. Another deceptively simple izakaya dish (Japanese pub food). Sure beats beer nuts.

1 lb (450 g) shimeji
   mushrooms, bottom
   spongy ends trimmed
   (mushrooms will separate)
2 Tbsp (30 mL) unsalted
   butter, cut into small pieces
Zest of 2 lemons
Low-sodium soy sauce,
   to serve

Cut out 2 sheets of aluminum foil, about 12 by 10 inches (30 × 25 cm) each.

Place the mushrooms in the centre of each sheet of foil, and sprinkle with the lemon juice as well as some salt and freshly ground pepper. Dot with the pieces of butter. Fold up the long sides and crease together at the top, leaving room for air to circulate inside, then close the packet on the right and left sides.

Preheat the grill to medium. Once preheated, place the packets on grill. Grill for 10 to 15 minutes, or until the packet is plump.

Transfer the packets onto serving plates, and cut a slit in the top of the foil with a sharp knife, being careful of the released steam. A dash of soy sauce at serving time makes this dish extra delicious.

JULIENNED POTATOES WITH MENTAIKO

Serves 4 to 6 as an appetizer

The Japanese answer to french fries, except that a short and gentle deep-fry ensures the potatoes stay white. Spicy cod roe, or *mentaiko*, is de rigueur in Japan, but any fish roe will do in a pinch. If you have a cast iron platter, preheat it in the oven so that the potatoes sizzle at the table.

4 medium russet potatoes

Vegetable oil for deep-frying, about 3 cups (750 mL)

2 Tbsp (30 mL) butter

2 Tbsp (30 mL) spicy cod roe (mentaiko) or your favourite fish roe

If using cod roe, use a sharp knife to cut open the outer membrane of the cod roe sac, and carefully scrape out the roe with a knife or small spoon. Keep cold.

Peel and cut the potatoes into a ¼-inch (6 mm) julienne. Plunge in a large bowl of cold water to remove excess starch. Drain in a colander and dry well on paper towels.

In a wok or a heavy-bottomed medium saucepan, heat the oil to 350°F (177°C) over medium-high. Line a baking sheet with paper towels.

Quickly deep-fry the potatoes a portion at a time, stirring frequently until slightly softened yet al dente, about 2 minutes. Be careful not to brown. Drain on the paper towels. Season with salt and freshly ground pepper to taste.

Immediately arrange the potatoes on a serving plate. Place the butter and cod roe on top, and stir to incorporate the roe and melt the butter.

JAPANESE ROLLED EGG OMELETTE

Serves 4 to 6

Dashimaki tamago—maki means "rolled," tamago is "egg." You might need a few tries to get the technique down, but not only does practice make perfect, practice is edible and just as delicious. This layered omelette, sweetened with a bit of mirin, requires adding the egg mixture to the cooking surface little by little. Room-temperature eggs ensure fluffiness. Serve with freshly grated daikon, soy sauce, Japanese pickles, and rice.

6 medium-small eggs,
   at room temperature
1 Tbsp (15 mL) soy sauce
2 tsp (10 mL) dashi stock
   (see the tip on page 223)
1½ tsp (7.5 mL) mirin
   (Japanese cooking wine)
Grapeseed oil or vegetable oil

In a bowl, whisk the eggs, soy sauce, dashi stock, and mirin using chopsticks.

Heat a 9-inch (23 cm) nonstick skillet (or a rectangular Japanese egg pan) over medium-high heat. Pour a little oil on a folded-up paper towel, not too much to saturate it, and use it to wipe the pan.

Transfer the eggs into a measuring cup to make it easier to pour. Pour one-quarter of the eggs into the pan, tilting the pan to cover the entire bottom of the pan. When the egg is set on the bottom but still runny on top, gently roll the egg in the direction of the handle, using one or two heatproof spatulas or a pair of chopsticks.

Leaving the rolled omelette in the pan, rub the pan with the paper towel, making sure to get the portion underneath the omelette. Stir the egg mixture once with the chopsticks, and pour another one-quarter of the egg mixture into the pan, again tipping the pan to evenly cover the bottom, and lifting up the rolled omelette to allow the raw egg mixture to run underneath it.

When the bottom is set but the top is still runny, roll the cooked egg away from you, gathering up the semi-cooked egg layer as you roll.

Repeat 2 more times with the remaining egg mixture, building a larger and larger omelette roll.

This takes practice. The idea is to keep building up layers of egg. The first omelette will provide the core around which the second semi-runny egg layer will be rolled. And so on. All of this creates a pleasing circular pattern inside the cooked omelette, revealed once sliced.

Transfer to a cutting board and make 1-inch (2.5 cm) slices, and serve.

SPINACH GOMA-AE
Serves 4

The name of this recipe literally means "spinach dressed with sesame seeds." If you think that sounds easy, well, it is! As with most Japanese dishes, it's just a few simple ingredients that make for a complex flavour punch.

1 lb (450 g) fresh spinach, washed well, stems kept on
¼ cup (60 mL) sesame seeds, plus more for garnish
2 Tbsp (30 mL) granulated sugar (optional)
2 Tbsp (30 mL) sake
1½ Tbsp (22.5 mL) soy sauce

Have ready a large bowl of ice water. Bring a large pot of water to a boil over high heat. Boil the spinach for about 30 seconds, or until it just wilts and is still a vibrant green colour. Using a slotted spoon or spider, immediately plunge into the bowl of ice water. Allow spinach to cool completely.

Drain the spinach, and squeeze it to remove excess water. Chop the spinach into 2- to 2½-inch (5–6 cm) lengths, and set aside.

Place the sesame seeds in a blender or food processor and grind until powdery. Add the sugar, if using, and blend. Add the soy sauce and sake, and then process until combined.

In a bowl, coat the boiled spinach with the sesame-seed dressing. Serve drizzled with the dressing and garnished with whole sesame seeds.

EDAMAME

Serves 2 to 4 as a snack or appetizer

Edamame are green soybeans still in the shell, quickly blanched in salt water and tossed in a bit of sea salt to make for an irresistible (and healthy) snack. These days you can find them in most grocers' frozen veggie section.

4 cups (1 L) frozen edamame
1 tsp (5 mL) kosher salt
Fleur de sel or your favourite crunchy salt, to taste

Bring a large pot of water to a boil over high heat. Add the salt and the edamame, and cook for 1 minute, or just until the edamame is heated through.

Drain using a colander. Shake off the excess water, and transfer to a serving plate. Sprinkle with fleur de sel (or your favourite salt) while still hot. Don't forget to leave out a bowl for the edamame shells.

SHOYU TAMAGO
Makes 8

You may be familiar with these soy-pickled eggs from the ramen shop. Super-simple Japanese pub food where the soy gives the egg a dark tinge.

8 large eggs, at room temperature

¾ cup (185 mL) soy sauce

Place the eggs in a large saucepan, and add cold water to cover the eggs by at least 1 inch (2.5 cm). Slowly bring the water to boil over medium heat; when the water reaches a boil, cook for 1 minute. Remove the pan from the heat, cover, and let sit for 12 minutes. Have ready a bowl of ice water.

Transfer the eggs to the bowl with ice water. When the eggs are cool, gently crack the shells by rapping and rolling the eggs on a cutting board. Put the eggs back in the cold water for a few more minutes, then peel. Try to get to the inner membrane, running your thumb under the membrane to feel the shiny white egg.

Lay the peeled eggs on a dry tea towel. Pat dry, then place the eggs in a large resealable freezer bag. Pour in the soy sauce, distribute the eggs evenly in the bag, and press out as much air as you can. Roll up bag to create a tight cylinder.

Refrigerate overnight, turning halfway to evenly distribute the soy.

Serve as a starter with drinks or as a side dish for a barbecue or picnic. Best the first day.

YAKI ONIGIRI
Makes 4 to 6 onigiri

People can get addicted to these little rice balls (okay, more triangles than balls, really). We like them seared instead of grilled, with butter and a little soy sauce. Adding oil to the frying pan raises the smoking point and prevents the butter from burning, and you get a nice crunchy exterior. Bonito is tuna that's been dried, smoked, and made into flakes. It seasons all sorts of dishes as well as cooking components such as flavourful dashi stock.

½ cup (125 mL) bonito flakes (katsuobushi)

1½ tsp (7.5 mL) soy sauce, for the filling

3 cups (750 mL) freshly cooked Japanese rice, cooled until easy to handle

2 Tbsp (30 mL) vegetable oil

1½ tsp (7.5 mL) butter

1 Tbsp (15 mL) soy sauce, for brushing the onigiri

4 sheets roasted nori (dried seaweed), cut into strips, for garnish

In a small bowl, mix the bonito with the soy sauce.

Have a bowl of water ready as well as a mini bowl of salt. Dip your hands in the water, and rub a bit of salt on them. Place a handful of rice in one hand, and press and form into a triangle about 1 inch (2.5 cm) thick. Make a well in the middle, and put in the bonito mixture. Close the well. Press the rice further so that the triangle becomes ¾ inch (2 cm) thick. Repeat with the remaining rice.

Place a medium nonstick skillet over medium-low heat. Add the vegetable oil and butter, and let the butter melt. Cook the onigiri for 4 to 5 minutes per side, or until lightly browned. (Watch carefully because it will burn quickly!) Brush the surface with the soy sauce, and cook for another 30 to 60 seconds. Repeat for the other side.

Serve garnished with the nori.

OKONOMIYAKI

Serves 2 to 3

This savoury shrimp, cabbage, and bacon pancake is a great way to start a meal, or served as a main course, especially with the warm daikon salad on page 223. Kewpie mayonnaise is a must-have Japanese condiment and worth looking for, but good ol' regular mayo will do. Other classic condiments for okonomiyaki: tonkatsu sauce, bonito flakes, and the red pickled ginger known as *beni shoga*.

1 cup (250 mL) all-purpose
    flour
2 cups (500 mL) dashi stock
    (see the tip on page 223)
2 large eggs, beaten
4 cups (1 L) green cabbage or
    napa cabbage, thinly sliced
¾ cup (185 mL) chopped
    raw shrimp (peeled
    and deveined)
8 green onions, white
    and green parts
    separated, sliced
8 slices raw bacon, cut in half
2 Tbsp (30 mL) vegetable oil,
    divided

TO SERVE
Kewpie mayonnaise or
    regular mayonnaise
Tonkatsu sauce
Toasted sesame seeds
Red pickled ginger
    (beni shoga)

In a large bowl, whisk together the flour, dashi, and eggs using chopsticks. Mix in the cabbage well. Fold in the shrimp and the sliced white part of the green onions, then season with salt.

Line a baking sheet with paper towels.

Heat 1½ teaspoons (7.5 mL) vegetable oil in a large nonstick skillet over medium-high heat until shimmering. Add ½ cup (125 mL) of the batter, gently spreading out the batter with a heatproof spatula. Form another pancake beside it in the pan. Cook until the underside is browned, about 4 minutes, then place 2 pieces of halved bacon on the top side.

Gently flip the pancakes so that the side with the bacon is now cooking. Cook until the bacon is crisp and the pancake is cooked through, about 5 more minutes. Drain on the paper towels. Repeat with the remaining batter and bacon.

Serve immediately with the mayonnaise, tonkatsu sauce, reserved green onions, and sesame seeds, with the pickled ginger on the side.

CHAWANMUSHI
Serves 4

Chawanmushi is loosely translated to "steamed in a cup." It's a savoury custard served as part of a meal (not a dessert). The combination of sweet shrimp, meaty chicken thighs, and earthy mushrooms in a silky-smooth egg custard is an eye-popper the first time you make it.

4 shrimp (21/25 count),
   peeled and deveined,
   sliced lengthwise
2 small skinless,
   boneless chicken thighs,
   cut into bite-size pieces
4 to 5 fresh shiitake
   mushrooms, sliced
1 tsp (5 mL) sake
1 tsp (5 mL) soy sauce,
   for the marinade
3 large eggs
2 cups (500 mL) dashi stock
   (see the tip on page 223)
1 tsp (5 mL) soy sauce,
   for the eggs
1 tsp (5 mL) mirin (Japanese
   cooking wine)
½ tsp (2.5 mL) kosher salt
2 green onions, thinly
   sliced on the bias

EQUIPMENT
Four 1-cup (250 mL)
   ovenproof ramekins
Large bamboo steamer
   basket with lid
   (large enough to
   fit the ramekins)

In a medium bowl, place the shrimp, chicken, and mushrooms, then add the sake and 1 teaspoon (5 mL) of the soy sauce. Mix to combine, then leave in the refrigerator to marinate for 1 hour.

In a medium bowl, whisk together the eggs, dashi, 1 teaspoon (5 mL) soy sauce, mirin, and salt. Strain through a fine-mesh sieve into a large measuring cup, straining through as much of the mixture as you can.

Divide the chicken, shiitake, and shrimp mixture evenly into the ramekins, then pour in the egg mixture to fill three-quarters of the ramekin. Cover each ramekin with aluminum foil and transfer to the steamer.

Place the steamer over a wok or large pot filled with moderately simmering water, and steam for about 20 minutes, periodically checking the water level. Check doneness with a bamboo skewer; when poked, a clear broth should come pouring out.

Sprinkle with green onions, and cover to steam for another 2 to 3 minutes.

Serve warm or cold.

TEBASAKI KARAAGE
Serves 4 (5 separated wings per person)

Pubs, or izakayas, are huge in Japan. When you cram 127 million people into such a small space, everyone needs a place to have a few drinks and blow off some steam. Good pub food is the perfect denouement of a long day. This is the izakaya version of the chicken wing. Potato flour makes these light and crispy.

---

10 chicken wings (or 20 wings and drumettes if already separated)
2 Tbsp (30 mL) soy sauce
2 Tbsp (30 mL) sake
2 Tbsp (30 mL) mirin (Japanese cooking wine)
½ tsp (2.5 mL) kosher salt
1 tsp (5 mL) finely grated garlic
1 tsp (5 mL) finely grated fresh ginger
½ cup (125 mL) potato flour
Vegetable oil for deep-frying, about 4 cups (1 L)

You can keep the chicken wings whole, or separate them into 2 parts, wings and drumettes, by cutting through the joint using a heavy knife. Remove the wing tips (discard or save for stock).

Mix the soy sauce, sake, mirin, salt, garlic, and ginger in a large bowl or a resealable plastic bag. Add the chicken, cover or seal, and leave to marinate in the fridge for 1 hour.

In a bowl, mix the potato flour with some salt and freshly ground pepper.

When ready to deep-fry, lift the chicken pieces from the marinade, then coat with the flour. In a wok or heavy-bottomed pot over medium-high, heat the oil to 350°F (177°C). Line a baking sheet with paper towels.

Deep-fry for 7 to 8 minutes, depending on the size of the chicken wing, occasionally turning them over using chopsticks. Remove with chopsticks or a slotted spoon or spider, and drain on the paper towels.

Pork, shrimp, and vegetable gyoza.

GYOZA
Serves 4 to 6 (makes 30 gyoza)

People the world over have figured out the delight of the dumpling. The Japanese version is gyoza, what was originally pot stickers in China. Gyoza can be pan-fried, deep-fried, or steamed; traditionally, they are pan-fried *and* steamed in the same pan. We've selected three different fillings for you to try out.

PORK GYOZA FILLING

1 cup (250 mL) finely
   chopped cabbage

1 tsp (5 mL) kosher salt

½ lb (220 g) ground pork

4 to 5 green onions,
   finely chopped

1 to 2 cloves garlic,
   finely grated

2 Tbsp (30 mL) soy sauce

1½ Tbsp (22.5 mL) sake

1 Tbsp (15 mL) sesame oil

DIPPING SAUCE

3 Tbsp (45 mL) soy sauce

3 Tbsp (45 mL) rice vinegar

1 tsp (5 mL) chili oil (rayu)
   or sesame oil

FOR FORMING AND FRYING THE GYOZA

Cornstarch, for dusting
   the baking sheet

Gyoza wrappers (dumpling
   wrappers)—30 for the pork
   gyoza, 30 for the shrimp
   gyoza (page 248), and
   15 to 20 for the vegetable
   gyoza (page 248)

3 to 4 Tbsp (45–60 mL)
   vegetable oil, for frying

PORK GYOZA FILLING: Place the cabbage in a colander set over a bowl. Toss the cabbage with the salt, and let sit for 10 minutes. Squeeze the excess moisture from the cabbage, and place in a large bowl. Add the pork, green onions, garlic, soy sauce, sake, and sesame oil, and mix well.

DIPPING SAUCE: Mix the 3 ingredients together in a small bowl.

FOR THE GYOZA: Lightly dust a baking sheet with cornstarch, and fill a tiny bowl with water for dipping your fingers in.

Take a sheet of gyoza wrapper in your hand, and place a tablespoon or so of the filling in the centre of the wrapper. With a finger dipped in water, moisten the edge along the lower half of the wrapper. As you close up the gyoza in a half-moon, fold a little pleat on one of the sides before sealing it closed; you'll be making about 6 pleats in total, while the other side stays smooth. Make sure the edges are sealed together well. Place on the cornstarch-dusted baking sheet. Keep the gyoza covered with a light tea towel or plastic wrap as you form the rest of the gyoza.

(Another way to form gyoza is to simply press the 2 edges together, and then fold the edge into pleats.)

Place a medium nonstick pan over medium-high heat. Have ready a lid that fits over the pan. Add 1 tablespoon (15 mL) of oil to the pan, and heat for about 1 minute. In batches, fry the gyoza until the bottoms become golden brown. Add ⅓ cup (80 mL) water and immediately cover with the lid, cooking for 3 to 4 more minutes or until the water evaporates. Transfer to a serving plate, and continue with the rest of the gyoza.

Serve immediately with the dipping sauce.

SHRIMP GYOZA
Serves 4 to 6 (makes 30 gyoza)

12 oz (340 g) shrimp, peeled and
  deveined
1 cup (250 mL) finely chopped nira
  (Chinese chives)
½ cup (125 mL) finely chopped canned
  water chestnuts
1½ Tbsp (22.5 mL) soy sauce
1½ Tbsp (22.5 mL) sake
1 Tbsp (15 mL) sesame oil
2 Tbsp (30 mL) cornstarch
30 gyoza wrappers (dumpling
  wrappers)

DIPPING SAUCE
3 Tbsp (45 mL) soy sauce
3 Tbsp (45 mL) rice vinegar
1 tsp (5 mL) chili oil (rayu) or sesame oil

Coarsely chop one-third of the shrimp with
a knife. Mince the remaining two-thirds in a
food processor. Transfer all the shrimp to a
large bowl. Add the nira, water chestnuts, soy
sauce, sake, sesame oil, and cornstarch, and
mix well.

Proceed with the third step of the main
gyoza recipe.

For the dipping sauce, mix the
3 ingredients together in a small bowl.

VEGETABLE GYOZA
Serves 3 to 4 (makes 15 to 20 gyoza)

You'll find ponzu sauce sold in
bottles at the Japanese food shop.
Sometimes you'll find a picture of a
yuzu, the citrus that ponzu is made
of, on the label.

1 cup (250 mL) chopped napa cabbage
1 tsp (5 mL) kosher salt
1½ cups (375 mL) mixed mushrooms
  such as shiitake, enoki, and oyster
½ cup (125 mL) finely chopped water
  chestnuts
1 tsp (5 mL) finely grated fresh ginger
1 Tbsp (15 mL) sake
1 tsp (5 mL) soy sauce
½ tsp (2.5 mL) sesame oil
15 to 20 gyoza wrappers (dumpling
  wrappers)

DIPPING SAUCE
1 Tbsp (15 mL) ponzu
2 Tbsp (30 mL) sesame oil
1 tsp (5 mL) chili oil

Place the cabbage in a colander set over a
bowl, and mix in the salt. Allow to drain for
10 minutes.

Squeeze out the excess water from the
cabbage, and place in a large bowl. Finely
chop the mushrooms, and add to the bowl,
along with the water chestnuts, ginger, sake,
soy sauce, and sesame oil.

Proceed with the third step of the main
gyoza recipe.

For the dipping sauce, mix the 3 ingredients together in a small bowl.

AGEDASHI TOFU
Serves 3 to 4

We couldn't do a show about Japanese cuisine without tofu. Here we deep-fry the firm variety to a crispy golden brown (helped by the magic of potato starch), and serve it with red chili relish and classic tempura sauce.

DAIKON AND RED-CHILI RELISH

1 cup (250 mL) finely grated fresh daikon (as finely grated as you can)

1 tsp (5 mL) red chili flakes or 1 red bird's eye chili, finely chopped

FOR THE SAUCE

¾ cup (185 mL) dashi stock (see the tip on page 223)

3 Tbsp (45 mL) low-sodium soy sauce

3 Tbsp (45 mL) mirin (Japanese cooking wine)

½ cup (125 mL) bonito flakes (katsuobushi)

FOR THE TOFU

1 block firm tofu, about 10 oz (285 g)

Potato flour, for coating the tofu

Vegetable oil for deep-frying, about 4 cups (1 L)

4 green onions, thinly sliced on the bias

2 sheets nori (dried seaweed), cut into thin strips using scissors

Make the daikon and red-chili relish first so that the flavours infuse. Place the daikon in a fine-mesh sieve over a bowl, and squeeze out the excess moisture. Mix it with the chili flakes (or fresh chili) right in the sieve. Set aside.

Make the sauce. Place the dashi, soy, and mirin in a medium saucepan, and bring to a simmer over medium heat. Add the bonito flakes and let it simmer for 3 minutes. Strain and keep warm.

In a heavy-bottomed pot or wok, heat the oil over medium-high heat to 350°F (177°C). Line a baking sheet or large plate with paper towels.

Slice the tofu into 8 pieces, and pat dry using paper towels. Place the potato flour in a bowl or dish, and add the tofu a few pieces at a time to cover with the starch. Deep-fry the tofu, turning it over a few times until the surface is golden and crispy, about 5 minutes. With a slotted spoon or spider, transfer the tofu onto the paper towels to drain.

Place the tofu in a serving bowl, and pour over some of the sauce. Garnish with the green onions, daikon and red-chili relish, and nori.

HAND-ROLLED SUSHI

Makes 15 to 20 small hand-rolls

Hand rolls (temaki) don't require sushi mats or years of practice. They're fun and easy to make at home and are a perfect first course to any fancy dinner party; they're also a great way to introduce sushi to kids. For the rice, make sure you use Japanese sushi rice; no other rice will do. There may be a few items you'll have to go to the Japanese grocery store for beforehand.

SUSHI RICE

2 cups (500 mL) Japanese sushi rice (uncooked)

2½ cups (625 mL) cold water, to cook the rice

1 piece of kombu (dried kelp), 2 by 2 inches (5 × 5 cm), wiped with a damp cloth

¼ cup (60 mL) rice vinegar

2 Tbsp (30 mL) granulated sugar

1 tsp (5 mL) kosher salt

HAND-ROLLED SUSHI

About 2 lbs (900 g) assorted sushi-grade fish (such as tuna, salmon, and shrimp), cut for sashimi (¼-inch/6 mm slices)

3 Tbsp (45 mL) finely chopped green onions or chives

2 Tbsp (30 mL) pickled ginger (gari), or more to taste

2 Tbsp (30 mL) wasabi paste

About 20 sheets nori (dried seaweed), cut into quarters

Soy sauce, for serving

Small handful of daikon sprouts, for serving (optional)

SUSHI RICE: Place the rice in a bowl. Working in the sink, add cold water to the rice, and stir in a circular motion using your hands, in only one direction so as not to break or damage the rice. Empty the bowl of most of the water, and repeat the rinsing and emptying until the water runs clear.

Strain the rice and transfer to a heavy-bottomed medium saucepan that has a tight-fitting lid. Add the cold water and kelp to the pan. Bring to a boil, then remove the kelp (discard). Reduce the heat to low, cover tightly, and cook until the water is absorbed and the rice is just tender, about 10 minutes.

While the rice cooks, in a small bowl combine the vinegar, sugar, and salt, and stir to dissolve.

Remove the pot of rice from the heat. Transfer the rice to a large baking sheet. With one hand, turn the rice gently using a wooden spoon, and with the other, sprinkle on the vinegar mixture and fan the rice to help it cool. Use very soon after making.

HAND-ROLLED SUSHI: Set a dinner plate, chopsticks, and a small saucer for each person who will be sitting at the table, and pour a little soy sauce into the saucer.

Arrange the slices of sashimi on a cold serving platter. Mound the green onions (or chives) and pickled ginger in a spot near the edge of the platter, and dab some wasabi in a free corner. Put the shiso leaves and nori separately on small plates. Put the sushi rice in a medium-size serving bowl. Bring everything to the table.

To make your own hand roll, lay a piece of nori, shiny side down, across your palm, and spread some rice on the nori, making sure not to overstuff. Using chopsticks, pick up a couple pieces of sashimi and drape them over the rice. Scrape some wasabi on the rice, and sprinkle with green onions (or chives) and/or daikon sprouts.

Roll into a cone shape, dip into the soy sauce, and enjoy! Refresh your palate between bites with the pickled ginger.

HAMACHI SASHIMI ON HOT RICE WITH DASHI

Serves 4

The secret here is to get the best-quality yellowtail tuna you can find (sushi-grade, of course). Salmon or shrimp sashimi would work too. It's a beautiful dish to look at and remarkable in its simplicity. Three simple ingredients with a small garnish on top—quintessentially Japanese.

1⅓ cups (330 mL) dashi stock (see the tip on page 223)

2 cups (500 mL) freshly cooked Japanese rice

16 slices yellowtail sashimi

4 tsp (20 mL) chives or thinly sliced green onions (green parts only)

½ sheet nori (dried seaweed), snipped into fine threads for sprinkling

Heat the dashi in a small saucepan just until warm over medium heat.

Scoop the hot rice into 4 small serving bowls (with a wooden rice paddle if you have one). Lay 4 slightly overlapping sashimi slices over the rice in each bowl.

Pour in the hot dashi to almost come up to the top of the rice (about ⅓ cup/80 mL). Sprinkle with the chives (or green onions) and nori, and serve immediately.

MISO SOUP

Serves 4

A standard that's served alongside pretty much any Japanese meal. Easy to master, and you can easily add ingredients to make this wonderful broth your own, even any vegetable you have left in the fridge (carrots, celery, and red peppers all work). We often make the two variations listed below the recipe.

2 tsp (10 mL) dashi stock
    powder (dashi no moto)
4 cups (1 L) water
3 Tbsp (45 mL) white or
    red miso paste
1 package (8 oz/220 g)
    silken tofu, cut into
    ½-inch (1 cm) cubes
2 green onions, sliced
    diagonally into ½-inch
    (1 cm) pieces

In a medium saucepan over medium-high heat, combine the dashi powder and water, and bring to a boil. Reduce the heat to medium, and whisk in the miso paste. Cook for 5 minutes.

Add the tofu and stir just until warmed through. Serve the soup garnished with green onions.

VARIATIONS

- Wakame is a soft seaweed that is sold dried. Just sprinkle 1 teaspoon (5 mL) of it in each bowl before garnishing with the green onions. It will take just a moment to reconstitute.
- Mushrooms are also great in miso soup. Add ½ pound (220 g) enoki mushrooms, sliced fresh shiitake, and/or torn oyster mushrooms to the stock after the miso paste is added. Cook for 1 minute or until just tender, and then continue with the recipe.

MISO AND SAKE SABLEFISH WITH SAUTÉED BABY BOK CHOY

Serves 4

The miso and sake marinade not only flavours the delicate fish but gives it a lovely burnt-orange hue when cooked. This dish needs at least an overnight marinade. Great with this simple sautéed bok choy, and steamed rice, of course. *Hajikami* is preserved ginger shoot, where half the long stalks are dyed a fuchsia pink; use chives instead if you can't find it.

½ cup (125 mL) sake

½ cup (125 mL) mirin (Japanese cooking wine)

½ cup (125 mL) white miso paste

¼ cup (60 mL) granulated sugar

4 sablefish (black cod) fillets, about ½ lb (220 g) each, skin on and scaled

1 Tbsp (15 mL) vegetable oil, for frying

4 hajikami, diced, or 4 finely chopped chives, to serve

SAUTÉED BABY BOY CHOY

1 lb (450 g) baby bok choy (about 12), woody bottoms removed, cut into 1-inch (2.5 cm) pieces (including the leaves)

1 Tbsp (15 mL) vegetable oil

1 tsp (5 mL) finely chopped fresh ginger

1 tsp (5 mL) finely chopped garlic

Juice of 1 lemon

Place the sake, mirin, miso, and sugar in a medium saucepan over medium heat, whisking to combine. Bring to a full simmer, then cook for 3 minutes to burn off the alcohol. Remove the pan from the heat, and let it cool completely. Refrigerate for at least 20 minutes.

Place the sablefish in a nonreactive container, and cover with the marinade. Cover the dish with plastic wrap, and leave to marinate in the refrigerator overnight and up to 2 days.

When ready to cook, preheat the oven to 400°F (200°C). Line a baking sheet with parchment paper. Remove the fish from marinade, just shaking off the excess.

Heat a large nonstick skillet over medium heat. Add the oil, and allow it to heat. Cook the fish flesh side down for 1 to 2 minutes, or until it becomes dark golden caramel colour. Using a metal fish spatula or flipper, turn over the fish, and slightly crisp the skin. Transfer the fish to the parchment-lined baking sheet, and bake for 15 to 20 minutes.

While the fish is cooking, prepare the bok choy. Place a large sauté pan over medium-high heat. Add the oil, and cook the garlic and ginger for 30 seconds or until fragrant but not browning. Add the bok choy, and stir-fry for 1 minute or just until heated through but still crispy. Season with salt and freshly ground pepper, and drizzle with the lemon juice. Remove the pan from heat.

Top the fish with the hajikami (or chives), and serve with the hot bok choy.

MISO OYSTER HOT POT
Serves 6

This is another wonderful family-style dish that the Japanese love so much. The unusual presentation comes from applying the miso paste to the sides of the serving pot to form a crust. Then, taking turns, everyone scrapes a bit into the pot as they scoop out the lovely poached oysters and mushrooms from the broth. Delicious *and* fun!

---

4 cups (1 L) shucked oysters, about 2¼ lbs (1 kg)

1 generous Tbsp (15 mL+) kosher salt

3 Japanese long onions (or 2 small leeks), washed and trimmed

2 bunches enoki mushrooms

10 to 12 fresh shiitake mushrooms, wiped clean and stems removed

¼ head napa cabbage

3 medium carrots

15 snow peas

6 Tbsp (90 mL) red miso paste

6 Tbsp (90 mL) white miso paste

1 Tbsp (15 mL) mirin (Japanese cooking wine)

4½ cups (1 L) dashi stock (see the tip on page 223), at room temperature, divided, plus more as needed

1 piece of kombu (dried kelp), 3 by 5 inches (8 × 12 cm)

Electric hot plate or gas burner

Toss the shucked oysters in salt and rinse under cold water.

Cut the long onions (or leeks) diagonally into 1½-inch (4 cm) lengths. If very thick, halve or quarter lengthwise before slicing diagonally.

Cut off the spongy ends of the enoki mushrooms, and leave in small bunches. Wipe the shiitake clean, remove the stems, and notch decorative crosses into the caps (or if large, simply cut in half).

Cut the cabbage crosswise into thin 1½-inch (4 cm) lengths. (The volume of cabbage will decrease by 80 to 90 percent when cooked.) Peel and cut the carrots into ¼-inch (6 mm) ribbons. Finally, add the snow peas, left whole, to the platter.

Heat about ½ cup (125 mL) of the dashi until warm. In a small bowl, mix the 2 types of miso together, using a fork or the back of a spoon. Add the mirin and the warm dashi to soften the miso; mix well. On the inside rim of a 9- or 10-inch (23 or 25 cm) shallow pot or skillet, spread the paste in a smooth layer using a rubber spatula, about ¼ inch (6 mm) thick and 2 inches (5 cm) wide. (Ideally you'd be using an earthenware casserole called a donabe, so please use it if you have one.)

Set up the hot plate (or gas burner) at the table, and place the pot or skillet on top. Score the kombu a few times with a knife so that its flavours release during cooking. Place it in the skillet, then pour in the remaining 4 cups (1 L) dashi. Bring it quickly to a boil over high heat, then reduce the heat to medium.

The vegetables and oysters may now be added to the simmering stock in whatever order you wish, a few servings at a time. The miso will not melt nor completely run into the stock; each diner scrapes as much miso as he or she wants into the dashi while scooping out a serving.

Take care not to overcook the oysters, or they will be tough; do these a few at time. Add more dashi, as needed.

No sauce accompanies this dish, but cooked morsels may be dipped in beaten egg in individual bowls.

SAKE-SIMMERED MACKEREL

Serves 4

Mackerel is an underappreciated fish in many parts of the world. Here it's mellowed out by simmering in sake and mirin with fresh ginger. Sake is available in single-serving bottles, so you don't have to buy a lot—though it's nice to drink with the mackerel.

¾ cup (185 mL) sake

4 portions mackerel fillet, about 4 oz (110 g) each, skin on but scaled and pin bones removed

½ cup (125 mL) mirin (Japanese cooking wine)

⅓ cup (80 mL) soy sauce

2 Tbsp (30 mL) julienned or slices of fresh ginger

Pinch of granulated sugar

Steamed Japanese rice, to serve

If you don't have a flat lid that's slightly smaller than the diameter of your medium-size heavy sauté pan, cut out a circle using parchment paper.

In the sauté pan, heat the sake over medium-high heat just until it reaches a simmer.

Lay the mackerel pieces in the pan, skin side up. Return to a simmer. Pour over the mirin, wait for it to come to a simmer, then add the soy sauce and sprinkle on the ginger and a pinch of sugar. (This staggered simmering helps to reduce the strong fish flavour of the mackerel.)

Cover with the small flat lid or parchment paper directly on top of the fish. Cook on high heat for about 8 minutes, or until the flesh has just lost its opaque colour and is cooked to your desired doneness. The cooking time will vary depending on the thickness.

Using a metal fish spatula, carefully transfer the fish to serving plates with rice. Drizzle with the sauce.

CLASSIC TEMPURA
Serves 4 to 6

Leave it to the Japanese to figure out how to make deep-fried food light and delicate. The secret to great tempura batter is to use cold bubbly water and to leave the batter a bit lumpy. If you can't find shemeji mushrooms, try enoki instead. In fact, try all sorts of different veggies (see note). Remember not to overcrowd the wok as the oil temperature will drop, resulting in soggy tempura.

DIPPING SAUCE
1 cup (250 mL) dashi stock
   (see the tip on page 223)
¼ cup (60 mL) low-sodium
   soy sauce
¼ cup (60 mL) mirin
   (Japanese cooking wine)
1 Tbsp (15 mL) sake

FOR THE BATTER
1 cup (250 mL) all-purpose
   flour
1 tsp (5 mL) kosher salt
1 large egg

1 Tbsp (15 mL) vegetable oil
1 cup (250 mL) cold
   sparkling water
½ cup (125 mL) ice
   water with ice

FOR THE TEMPURA
Cornstarch, for dredging
Vegetable oil for deep-frying,
   about 4 cups (1 L)
10 shrimp (21/25 count),
   peeled and deveined
   with tails left on

1 large carrot, peeled and cut
   diagonally into ¼-inch
   (6 mm) slices
1 Japanese eggplant, cut into
   ½-inch (1 cm) slices
10 snow peas, left whole
8 to 9 shiso leaves (optional)
10 fresh shiitake
   mushrooms,
   stems removed
1 bunch shimeji
   mushrooms, separated
   into small bunches

For the dipping sauce, bring the dashi to a boil in a small saucepan over medium-high heat. Add the soy sauce, mirin, and sake, then reduce the heat and simmer for a few minutes. Remove the pan from the heat and keep warm.

Make the tempura batter. Sift together the flour and salt in a small bowl. In a medium bowl, beat the egg with the vegetable oil using chopsticks, then add the sparkling water and the ice water along with the ice. Add the flour all at once, and stir briefly, just enough to combine. The batter should be lumpy and slightly thinner than pancake batter.

Line a plate with paper towels, and fill a bowl with cornstarch. In a wok or heavy-bottomed pot, heat the oil to 325°F (163°C) over medium-high heat.

Holding the shrimp by the tail, dredge the shrimp, shaking off the excess, then dip into the batter, again shaking off the excess. Immediately drop into the hot oil. Continue with the remaining shrimp. Deep-fry until they are crispy and barely golden brown, 1 to 2 minutes. Remove from the oil using chopsticks, a slotted spoon, or a spider, and drain on the paper towels.

Do the same for the vegetables, dredging in cornstarch and dipping in batter, except using chopsticks this time. Deep-fry until golden brown and crispy.

Serve immediately with dipping sauce.

NOTE:
Also try making tempura with bell peppers, enoki mushrooms, zucchini, broccoli florets, daikon, and green onions.

JAPANESE CURRY AND RICE

Serves 6 to 8

The recipe name pretty much says it all. You probably don't think of curry when you think of Japanese food but there are many influences on modern Japanese cuisine. Take a peek at the recipe and you'll note that the curry is considerably sweeter than the Indian or Thai versions with the addition of apples and apricot jam.

1½ lbs (670 g) beef sirloin, cut into 1-inch (2.5 cm) cubes

1 Tbsp (15 mL) vegetable oil

1 Tbsp (15 mL) all-purpose flour

2 Spanish onions, finely diced

3 cloves garlic, finely chopped

2 tsp (10 mL) finely chopped fresh ginger

3 carrots, peeled and cut in medium dice

15 baby potatoes, cut in half

1 Tbsp (15 mL) tomato paste

3 Tbsp (45 mL) curry powder

3 cups (750 mL) beef stock

2 tsp (10 mL) Worcestershire sauce

1 Tbsp (15 mL) apricot jam

1 medium apple, peeled and cut into matchsticks, for garnish

Steamed Japanese rice, to serve

Thousand-Slice Turnip Pickle (page 216), for garnish (optional)

Line a large plate or baking sheet with paper towels. Season the beef with salt and freshly ground pepper. Heat a large sauté pan over medium heat, and add the vegetable oil. Brown the beef, turning until a deep caramel colour on all sides, about 5 minutes. Sprinkle the flour over the meat to coat. Remove the pan from the heat, and transfer the beef onto the paper towels. Set aside.

In the same pan, add the onion, garlic, and ginger, and sauté for about 3 minutes over medium-high heat. Add the carrots and potatoes, and then the tomato paste and curry powder. Stir, deglazing the pan with the stock. Let it come to a simmer.

Add the reserved beef along with the Worcestershire, apricot jam, and some salt and freshly ground pepper. Cook, simmering until the potatoes are cooked and the meat is fork tender, 10 to 15 minutes. If necessary, add water to keep the beef and vegetables completely submerged.

Season with salt and freshly ground pepper, to taste. Serve with rice, and garnish with the apple and turnip pickle.

KIMCHI HOT POT
Serves 6

Kimchi, the deliciously spicy pickled cabbage from Korea, shows up in Japanese cooking too, and is widely available at Asian markets. It's spicy, sweet, crunchy, and tart all at once and gives this hot pot an indescribably delicious aroma. As previously mentioned, negi looks like a longer and thicker green onion and has a lovely sweet flavour, easily substituted with regular green onions or small leeks. Use any combination of vegetables you like; bok choy and enoki are also great in this dish. If you have a hot plate or gas burner, bring the pot to the table so that everyone can serve themselves in true hot-pot style.

½ lb (220 g) skinless, boneless chicken breasts or ground chicken

1 small pork belly, about 10 oz (300 g), rind removed, or ground pork

2 tsp (10 mL) finely grated or finely chopped fresh ginger

1 large egg

1 Tbsp (15 mL) sake

1 Tbsp (15 mL) soy sauce

1 Tbsp (15 mL) potato flour

3 cups (750 mL) chicken stock

3 Tbsp (45 mL) white miso paste

1 Tbsp (15 mL) soy sauce

1½ tsp (7.5 mL) granulated sugar

1 cup (250 mL) store-bought kimchi

2 medium carrots, peeled and cut into ¼-inch (6 mm) slices or finely diced

1 negi, or 2 green onions or half leek, cut into 1½-inch (4 cm) lengths

15 unpeeled baby potatoes, blanched and sliced in half

10 to 15 fresh shiitake mushrooms, stems removed

Freshly grated daikon, for garnish (optional)

Finely chop the chicken and the pork belly (if not using ground chicken or pork), and place in a medium bowl. Add the ginger, egg, sake, soy sauce, and potato flour. Mix well with your hands until evenly incorporated. Form into 1½-inch (4 cm) meatballs.

In a large pot (an earthenware pot if you have one), add the chicken stock, miso, soy sauce, and sugar, and bring to a simmer over medium heat. Add the meatballs and kimchi, cover, and cook for 10 minutes.

Add the carrots, negi (or green onions or leek), potatoes, and shiitake, and cook for a further 15 minutes. serve with steamed rice and garnish with grated daikon.

TERIYAKI STEAK

Serves 1 to 2, and makes about 2 cups (500 mL) teriyaki sauce

Once you've made your own teriyaki sauce, you'll never buy the store-bought stuff again. Put it on steaks, chicken, veggies—anything. The secret to perfect steak on the stovetop is to get your skillet superhot; cast iron is best.

TERIYAKI SAUCE

½ cup (125 mL) soy sauce

½ cup (125 mL) mirin (Japanese cooking wine)

¼ cup (60 mL) granulated sugar

1½ tsp (7.5 mL) cornstarch

½ cup (125 mL) water

FOR THE STEAK

½ lb (220 g) sirloin steak, 1 inch (2.5 cm) thick

Extra-virgin olive oil, for drizzling

1 Tbsp (15 mL) extra-virgin olive oil, for searing

TERIYAKI SAUCE: Add the soy sauce, mirin, and sugar to a small saucepan. In a small bowl, dissolve the cornstarch in the water, then add the slurry to the pan. Cook, whisking constantly, over medium-low heat, or until slightly thickened and all the sugar has dissolved. Remove the pan from the heat.

FOR THE STEAK: Season the steak with salt and freshly ground pepper, and drizzle with olive oil.

Preheat a cast iron skillet over medium-high heat. Add the 1 tablespoon (15 mL) olive oil to the pan, and then the steak. Cook without moving until a dark crust is formed, about 4 to 5 minutes. Turn over the steak, and cook until desired doneness, another 4 to 5 minutes for medium-rare.

Let rest on a plate, and tent with aluminum foil. Pour some teriyaki sauce over the steak, and enjoy.

TATSUTA-FRIED CHICKEN WITH ZUCCHINI CHIPS
Serves 4 as an appetizer

This is similar to the chicken wing recipe on page 244 but without the indelicacy of the bones to deal with. We find chicken thighs to be considerably more tender and flavourful than the more popular breast meat. The sake and soy marinade ensure that the meat stays juicy, and the potato starch gives each bite a light, flaky texture.

1 medium zucchini
1¼ lbs (570 g) skin-on, boneless chicken thighs
1½ tsp (7.5 mL) kosher salt
3 Tbsp (45 mL) sake
¼ cup (60 mL) low-sodium soy sauce
1 cup (250 mL) potato flour
Vegetable oil for deep-frying, about 4 cups (1 L)
Lemon wedges, as garnish

Cut off the ends of the zucchini. Halve the zucchini crosswise, and using an apple corer, remove the seeds. Thinly slice the zucchini, and place on a paper towel–lined plate to dry out slightly. Set aside.

Cut the chicken into bite-size chunks, making sure to cut across the grain to result in a softer final texture. Transfer to a medium bowl, add the salt, and rub the salt in well with your hands. Add sake and continue rubbing the chicken. Set aside.

Place the soy sauce and potato flour in 2 separate bowls.

First fry the zucchini chips. In a heavy-bottomed pot or wok, heat the oil to 350°F (177°C) over medium-high heat. Line a large baking sheet with paper towels, for draining both the deep-fried zucchini and the chicken.

Add the zucchini and deep-fry until light golden brown and crispy (which should happen quite quickly). Remove using a slotted spoon or spider, and drain on the paper towels. Sprinkle with salt and freshly ground pepper.

Reduce the heat of the oil to 340°F (170°C). Using chopsticks, dip the chicken pieces in soy sauce, and then coat with the potato flour. In 2 or more separate batches, deep-fry the chicken, being careful not to overcrowd the pot. Cook, occasionally turning over the chicken using chopsticks, for 5 to 6 minutes, or until crispy, golden, and fully cooked. Remove using a slotted spoon or spider and let drain on the paper towels.

Arrange the chicken on a serving plate with the fried zucchini and lemon wedges. (Fresh lemon juice is essential to this dish!)

GREEN TEA ICE CREAM
Makes 1 quart (1 L)

Matcha is powdered Japanese green tea. With all the fancy tea shops popping up these days, you should have no problem finding it. It tints the ice cream a smooth subtle green and gives it a nice gentle bite.

2 cups (500 mL) heavy cream
1 cup (250 mL) whole milk
   (or half-and-half for
   creamier consistency)
¼ tsp (1 mL) kosher salt
6 large yolks
⅔ cup (160 mL) granulated
   sugar
2 Tbsp (30 mL)
   matcha powder
Ice cream maker

GARNISHES (OPTIONAL)
Whipped cream
Japanese red bean paste
Cornflakes
Diced fresh fruit, such as
   oranges and cherries

Have ready a medium stainless-steel bowl sitting on top of another bowl with ice. Place a fine-mesh sieve in the top bowl.

In a medium heavy-bottomed pot, bring the cream, milk, and salt to a simmer over medium-low heat.

In a bowl, whisk together the eggs, sugar, and matcha. If the matcha does not completely dissolve, pour in about 1 cup (250 mL) of the hot cream mixture in a slow stream, whisking vigorously.

And the whisked-egg mixture into the pot with the cream. Cook, stirring constantly with a wooden spoon or heatproof spatula, over medium-low heat, until thick enough to coat the back of spoon, or registers 165°F (74°C) on an instant-read thermometer. Do not let it boil. Immediately pour the custard through the sieve into the stainless-steel bowl. Cool to room temperature, stirring occasionally. Chill, covered, until cold, at least 1 hour.

Freeze in the ice cream maker, following manufacturer's instructions. Transfer to an airtight container, and let it harden in the freezer.

Serve with whipped cream, and/or any other sundae garnishes of your choice.

THAILAND

Pailin Chongchitnant

I was always in the kitchen, as a child growing up in Thailand. My live-in nanny was also the cook of our family, and she never failed to delegate tasks whenever she'd find me the kitchen. First I was just grating fresh coconut or picking herbs from the garden, but soon the tasks became more complex and eventually I could make dishes from start to finish. And when either of my grandmothers came to visit, I'd be introduced to a whole new repertoire of recipes and cooking techniques. Without my realizing it, my nanny and both of my grandmothers were teaching me the art of Thai cuisine.

I was always intrigued by the sounds, the smells, and the action in the kitchen. I'd hear the granite mortar and pestle pounding a mixture of herbs or sense chilies in the air. I could feel the heat radiating from the inferno blazing underneath the wok. And there was always the smell of fresh limes being squeezed over a salad. Thai food captured all my senses, and there was no place I was happier than in our kitchen.

After graduating high school, I said goodbye to my family and headed for Vancouver. I had no idea how Canadians perceived Thailand, its people and its culture. I soon realized that the most common response to "I'm from Thailand" was going to be "Oh, I love Thai food!" At first I thought it was just a polite default response because they didn't know what else to say. But as I spent many meals at Thai restaurants together with friends who were the ones insisting we go there, I realized that Canadians *really* loved Thai food. "It's just so full of flavour," they'd say. And indeed, Thai food is bold—no doubt about it.

But as much as people love Thai food, few people I know cook it at home. They tell me that it seems so complicated, so intricate . . . so mysterious. And I have to say, this is exactly the same feeling I had about Western cuisine. All the ingredients were unfamiliar, cooking techniques were new, where do I even begin? But I dove in, and little by little, dish by dish, I grew more comfortable. And before I knew it, the fear and intimidation were

completely gone. I realized this was the natural process for anyone trying to learn a new cuisine, with all of its unfamiliarity. And it could all be overcome simply by cooking it one dish at a time. You have a new ingredient in front of you, and as you use it over and over, you don't think about it anymore. You just know how much fish sauce to add. And you'll probably wonder why you waited so long to get started.

One thing you may have heard about Thai dishes: they always feature some magical combination of salty, sweet, sour, and spicy, each dish a unique interpretation of the four flavours. There's always a lot going on in any single bite. The key to making delicious Thai food is striking the right balance, or what I call "the sweet spot," for each dish. But here's the secret: you're in control of where that sweet spot is. There's no one right answer or right way to cook a Thai dish. Thai food is so much fun to play around with! After cooking just a few dishes, you'll discover a few things, such as our heavy reliance on fresh herbs and bright flavours, and exactly how sweet balances salty and sour. And then you can tinker with the flavours however you like until an exact combination strikes a chord with you.

For those who haven't tried cooking Thai food, I encourage you to take that first leap and give it a go. Thai food is much simpler than it may seem. And it's exciting to experiment with the flavours, aromas, textures, and colours, all of which I find absolutely tantalizing to the senses. Our abundance of fresh herbs are like the different colours of paint on a palette; you'll come to see how versatile they are. And don't be afraid to use these new Thai ingredients in other dishes. Fish sauce may seem like it only belongs in Asian dishes, but it can also add extra personality to your beef stew! Your taste buds are going to be introduced to flavour combinations that are totally new and refreshing.

I spent the first twenty years of my life in Thailand, and I've gone back to visit every year since I left. The country's food still never fails to fascinate me. There is *still* so much to learn and discover. I am truly grateful that my nanny and my grandmothers let me join them in the kitchen and helped grow and nurture my passion for our cuisine. I invite you to experience and see why this cuisine has so deeply captivated me.

ด้วยรัก
Pailin

Recipes

DEEP-FRIED SPRING ROLLS
Makes 10 to 12 spring rolls (serves 5 to 6 as an appetizer)

Who doesn't love spring rolls? Saam-gler is a combination of garlic, cilantro roots, and peppercorns, used in Thai dishes to punch up flavour. Glass noodles are also called bean threads, mung bean vermicelli, or cellophane noodles—they are more translucent than noodles made with rice.

3 oz (85 g) glass noodles (vermicelli)

10 dried shiitake mushrooms

4 Tbsp (60 mL) vegetable oil, divided

7 oz (200 g) ground pork

1 Tbsp (15 mL) saam-gler (page 283)

3 cups (750 mL) napa cabbage, finely chopped

1 cup (250 mL) carrots, grated

1 Tbsp (15 mL) oyster sauce

1 Tbsp (15 mL) granulated sugar

1 tsp (5 mL) soy sauce

1 large egg

10 to 12 spring roll wrappers (8-inch/20 cm square wrappers)

Vegetable oil for deep-frying, about 5 cups (1.25 L)

Sweet and sour chili sauce (page 283) or chili jam (page 287), to serve

Soak the vermicelli in a bowl of cold water for 10 minutes, or until pliable. Drain the noodles in a colander, and cut into 1½-inch (4 cm) lengths.

In a small bowl, soak the mushrooms in warm water for 10 minutes. Squeeze out the water from the mushrooms, and cut off and discard the stems. Finely slice and set aside.

Heat 2 tablespoons (30 mL) of the oil in a wok or large skillet over medium heat, and cook the pork for 3 to 4 minutes, or until browned and any liquid that comes out evaporates. Strain in a sieve and set aside.

Heat the remaining 2 tablespoons (30 mL) oil in the wok or skillet over medium heat. Add the saam-gler, and cook for 1 minute or until fragrant. Add the reserved mushrooms, and stir-fry for 1 to 2 minutes or until fragrant. Reduce the heat to low, then add the cabbage and carrots and stir-fry for 1½ minutes. (Avoid overcooking, which will make the filling soggy.) Remove the wok from the heat. Add the reserved noodles and cooked ground pork, and then the oyster sauce, sugar, and soy sauce, plus a pinch of salt. Stir until thoroughly combined.

In a small bowl, lightly beat the egg. Lay a spring roll wrapper on the work surface with one of the corners facing you. Put 2 tablespoons (30 mL) of the filling in the centre. Fold the bottom corner up and over the filling, and then fold in the left and right corners. Roll up the package, and as you approach the top, lightly brush the top edges with the beaten egg to help seal the spring roll. Repeat with the rest of the filling, covering the formed spring rolls with a damp tea towel.

Line a baking sheet with paper towels. Heat the oil for deep-frying in a wok or heavy-bottomed pot to 375°F (191°C) over medium-high heat.

In batches, deep-fry the spring rolls in batches for 6 to 7 minutes until golden brown and crispy, then remove with a slotted spoon or spider and let drain on the paper towels.

Serve with the sweet and sour chili sauce (or chili jam).

SAAM-GLER
Makes 3 tablespoons (45 mL)
saam-gler

1 cup (250 mL) cilantro roots
4 cloves garlic
2 tsp (10 mL) black or
   white peppercorns

Pound the cilantro roots roughly in a mortar and pestle. Add the garlic, and continue to pound until the mixture starts to become paste-like. Finally, add the peppercorns and pound to a fine paste.

Keeps refrigerated for up to 3 weeks.

SWEET AND SOUR CHILI SAUCE
Makes 2 cups (500 mL) chili sauce

Move over ketchup. This is going to be the new condiment of choice chez vous.

1 cup (250 mL) rice vinegar
1 cup (250 mL) granulated sugar
2 Tbsp (30 mL) soy sauce
4 red bird's eye chilies, seeds removed,
   roughly chopped
1 Tbsp (15 mL) chopped garlic

Place all of the ingredients in a blender, and blend into a purée. Transfer the mixture to a saucepan, and cook over medium heat until it's slightly syrupy, 4 to 5 minutes.

Keeps refrigerated for 10 days.

STEAMED SPRING ROLLS

Makes 10 spring rolls

Here's the steamed version of the spring roll, which is just as popular as the deep-fried kind. We've gone all-vegetarian in this recipe, which features vermicelli noodles, carrots, bean sprouts, and cilantro. As always, feel free to substitute your own ingredients, but make sure they're all cut to the same size to ensure even steaming.

5 oz (140 g) dried
   rice vermicelli
1 cup (250 mL) grated carrot
½ cup (125 mL) fresh
   bean sprouts
3 Tbsp (45 mL) roughly
   chopped fresh cilantro
   leaves
2 Tbsp (30 mL) soy sauce
1 Tbsp (15 mL) fresh
   lime juice
1 Tbsp (15 mL) chili jam
   (page 287)
1½ tsp (7.5 mL) granulated
   sugar
1 Tbsp (15 mL) fried garlic
   (see the tip on page 304)
10 ten-inch (25 cm) dried
   rice paper wrappers
Sweet and Sour Chili Sauce
   (page 283), to serve
Bamboo steaming basket
   (with lid)

Soak the vermicelli in a bowl of cold water for 10 minutes or until softened.

In a large bowl, add the carrot, bean sprouts, and cilantro. Drain the vermicelli, and add to the bowl. Add the soy sauce, lime juice, chili jam, sugar, and fried garlic, and using your hands, mix until combined.

Fill a pie plate or shallow bowl with warm water. Working with one round of rice paper at a time, dip it into the water until it's pliable, then lay it flat on a large cutting board.

Put 1 to 2 tablespoons (15–30 mL) of filling in the centre of the rice paper, being careful not to overfill. Fold the bottom of the paper up and over the filling, then fold over the left and right sides. Roll up the package; it should stick to itself. Repeat until all the filling is used.

Line the bamboo steaming basket with parchment paper, and in a wok or large pot over which the steamer can fit, bring about 2 inches (5 cm) of water to a boil, then reduce the heat to medium.

Transfer the rolls into the basket, cover with the lid, and set it over the simmering water. Steam for 5 minutes, or until cooked.

Serve with the chili sauce.

. . . CONTINUED

CHILI JAM

Makes 2 cups (500 mL) chili jam

Chili jam is a must-have condiment in Thailand. It packs all the sweet, sour, salty, and spicy hits you'd expect in Thai food into a delicious jammy topping. What separates this concoction from your run-of-the-mill hot sauce is the subtle deep flavour of the shrimp paste. Make lots—it keeps well in the fridge. Use it whenever you're looking for a touch of heat.

Vegetable oil for deep-frying, about 1 cup (250 mL)

2 cups (500 mL) shallots, sliced lengthwise

1 cup (250 mL) garlic, sliced lengthwise

Five ⅛-inch (3 mm) slices unpeeled galangal

½ cup (125 mL) dried long red chilies, rinsed, seeds removed

¼ cup (60 mL) dried shrimp, rinsed and pat dry

½ tsp (2.5 mL) shrimp paste

½ cup (125 mL) palm sugar (chopped, pounded in a mortar and pestle, or finely grated)

2 Tbsp (30 mL) tamarind paste (page 312)

¼ cup (60 mL) fish sauce

In a wok or heavy-bottomed small saucepan over medium-high, heat the oil to 350°F (177°C) heat. Deep-fry the shallots, garlic, galangal, chilies, and dried shrimp until golden. Watch the chilies carefully; you want them to just blister and brown as burning will make the chili jam very bitter. Remove using a slotted spoon or spider, and leave to cool on a plate.

Transfer to a food processor, add the shrimp paste, and blend. Add some of the deep-frying oil if the mixture is dry.

Pour the mixture into a medium saucepan. Bring to a simmer over medium-high heat, and add the palm sugar, tamarind, and fish sauce until quite thick, 5 to 7 minutes.

Store in a glass jar in the fridge. Will keep for 10 days.

THAI SHRIMP CAKES

Makes 6 to 8 shrimp cakes (serves 3 to 4 as an appetizer)

Thailand's answer to the crab cake, using spicy and aromatic Thai red curry paste. Japanese panko breadcrumbs (widely available) are lighter and crispier than regular breadcrumbs. These are perfect with the sweet and sour dipping sauce on page 283 and the cucumber salad on page 299.

20 oz (565 g) shrimp,
    peeled and deveined

2 Tbsp (30 mL) Thai red
    curry paste (store-bought)

1 large egg yolk

6 yardlong green beans
    (or 12 regular green
    beans), trimmed and cut
    into ⅛-inch (3 mm) pieces

1 tsp (5 mL) finely chopped
    unpeeled galangal

3 lime leaves, centre vein
    removed and discarded,
    finely chopped

1 cup (250 mL) panko
    breadcrumbs

Vegetable oil for deep-frying,
    about 2 cups (500 mL)

¼ cup (60 mL) finely chopped
    peanuts, for garnish

Fresh sprigs of cilantro,
    for garnish

Finely chop the shrimp, using either a knife or a food processor. Transfer to a large bowl. Mix in the curry paste, then add the egg yolk, green beans, galangal, and lime leaves, and stir.

Have ready a baking sheet for the shaped shrimp cakes, and place the breadcrumbs on a plate. Form 6 to 8 shrimp cakes by taking a spoonful of the shrimp mixture and flattening it slightly. Dip it into the breadcrumbs to cover all sides, and lay on the parchment. Repeat with the rest of the shrimp mixture.

Line a baking sheet or large plate with paper towels. Heat the oil in a wok or heavy-bottomed pot over medium-high heat until the oil reaches somewhere between 325°F to 350°F (163°C–177°C). Deep-fry the shrimp cakes a few at a time until golden brown and crispy, about 2 to 3 minutes. Remove using a slotted spoon or spider. Drain on the paper towels.

Serve sprinkled with peanuts and cilantro sprigs.

THAI SMOKED-TROUT SALAD WITH GREEN MANGOES

Serves 4 to 6

The sweet smoked trout plays nicely off the tangy green (raw) papaya and nutty toasted rice. As with many Thai dishes, equal attention is paid to the topping and the dish itself. Here we feature basil, mint, and red chilies. This one looks stunning on the plate.

2 Thai eggplants, sliced into
   ½-inch (1 cm) rounds
4 shallots, unpeeled
4 cloves garlic, unpeeled
1-inch (2.5 cm) piece
   unpeeled galangal
Vegetable oil, for drizzling
1 Tbsp (15 mL) uncooked
   white sticky rice
   (also called sweet rice
   or glutinous rice) or
   jasmine rice
1 medium or 2 small green
   mangoes, peeled and
   grated or cut into ⅛-inch
   (3 mm) julienne
15 fresh Thai basil leaves,
   roughly torn
15 fresh mint leaves,
   roughly torn
2 long red bird's eye chilies,
   seeds removed,
   finely chopped or
   very finely sliced
2 Tbsp (30 mL) fresh
   lime juice
2 Tbsp (30 mL) fish sauce
7 oz (200 g) smoked
   trout fillet, flaked
Vegetable grilling basket

Preheat the grill to medium.

Drizzle the eggplants, shallots, garlic, and galangal lightly with the oil and place in a vegetable grilling basket. Grill the vegetables until charred and tender. Set aside.

Toast the rice in a small skillet over medium heat, stirring constantly until golden, about 4 to 5 minutes. Allow to cool. Grind to a powder using a spice grinder (or coffee grinder set aside for spices) or a mortar and pestle.

Peel the shallots and garlic and chop coarsely, and transfer to a large bowl. Slice the galangal (you don't have to peel it) and coarsely chop the eggplant, and add to the bowl. Add the mango, Thai basil, mint, and chilies, and stir to combine. Transfer to a serving platter.

In a small bowl, mix together the lime juice and fish sauce. Drizzle over the salad. Add the toasted rice and mix. Top the salad with the flaked trout.

GREEN PAPAYA SALAD WITH CRISPY PORK

Serves 2

In order to get succulent, crispy pork, you have to start this dish the day before you serve it. The tough pork shoulder has to marinate overnight in the sweet, salty, spicy syrup, which infuses the meat and tenderizes it. The salad features green papaya (a raw version of the sweet red one you're probably used to) that stands up to grating, and brings a nice texture to the salad. We also use dried shrimp (cheap and available at any decent Asian food store) pounding it into a paste with garlic, chilies, and peanuts. All of it results in a joyous flavour burst in your mouth. Enjoy!

CRISPY PORK

1 cup (250 mL) palm sugar (chopped, pounded in a mortar and pestle, or finely grated)

½ cup (125 mL) kecap manis (or Thai black/dark sweet soy sauce)

3 Tbsp (45 mL) oyster sauce

2 star anise

7 oz (200 g) boneless pork shoulder, cut into 2- by 1-inch pieces ⅛ inch thick (5 × 2.5 cm × 3 mm)

Vegetable oil for deep-frying, about 2 cups (500 mL)

FOR THE SALAD

3 cloves garlic

4 to 6 red bird's eye chilies

2 Tbsp (30 mL) dried shrimp

1 heaped Tbsp (15 mL+) roughly chopped roasted peanuts

1 slice of lime

8 cherry tomatoes, quartered

1 cup (250 mL) peeled green papaya, cut into matchsticks

FOR THE DRESSING

2 Tbsp (30 mL) finely grated or chopped palm sugar

1 to 2 Tbsp (15–30 mL) fish sauce

1 Tbsp (15 mL) fresh lime juice

1 Tbsp (15 mL) tamarind paste (page 312)

. . . CONTINUED

Start the marinade the night before. In a medium saucepan, place the palm sugar, kecap manis, oyster sauce, star anise, and a pinch of salt, and simmer and reduce until it becomes syrupy, about 5 minutes. Let the syrup cool.

Slice the pork into 2- by 1-inch (5 × 2 cm) pieces ⅛ inch (3 mm) thick. Place in a covered container with the palm sugar syrup, and leave in the refrigerator to marinate overnight.

The next day, drain the pieces of pork on a wire rack set over a plate, until most marinade had dripped off. This will avoid burning when you deep-fry the pork.

In a mortar and pestle, pound the garlic with the chilies and a pinch of salt. Add the shrimp and peanuts, and pound into a paste. Transfer to a large bowl.

Add the slice of lime and the cherry tomatoes, gently mashing with the pestle or wooden spoon. Add the papaya, slightly bruising it as you mix it with the rest of the ingredients. Discard the lime slice.

For the dressing, combine the palm sugar, fish sauce, lime juice, and tamarind in a small bowl, and mix until the sugar is dissolved. Toss the dressing with the salad.

Line a baking sheet with paper towels. In a wok or heavy-bottomed saucepan over medium-high, heat the oil to 350°F to 370°F (177°C–188°C).

Carefully add the pork to the oil. Deep-fry, turning over occasionally, until crispy and fragrant, with a colour to them. Remove using a slotted spoon or spider. Drain on the paper towels.

Serve on top of the papaya salad.

LAAB SALAD
Serves 3 to 4

Pork salad? You bet. It's a dish where ground pork finally gets to be centre stage. Toasted and ground rice is a common garnish for Thai salads; use sticky rice, which is also worth buying for the dessert on page 336. There are instructions below to adjusting the amount of lime juice and fish sauce; if you're new to Thai cooking, getting the right balance of flavours is a fun process of trial and error.

3 Tbsp (45 mL) uncooked white sticky rice (also called sweet rice or glutinous rice) or jasmine rice
1 to 2 limes, divided
½ lb (220 g) ground pork
2 green onions, thinly sliced
2 shallots, cut into ⅛-inch (3 mm) slices
10 sprigs fresh cilantro, roughly chopped
¼ cup (60 mL) torn fresh mint leaves
3 Tbsp (45 mL) fish sauce, plus more to taste
1 tsp (5 mL) red chili powder
1 head of butter lettuce or Boston lettuce (core removed, leaves left whole)
Fresh Thai basil, for garnish (optional)

Toast the rice in a small skillet over medium heat, stirring constantly until the rice is a rich golden colour, about 4 to 5 minutes. Allow to cool, then pound in a mortar and pestle or process in a spice grinder or coffee grinder until finely ground. Set aside.

Squeeze the juice from a lime half onto the ground pork. Mix it in well, and let it marinate for a few minutes.

Heat a large skillet over medium heat. Add 2 tablespoons (30 mL) of water to the pan, and immediately add the pork. Cook, stirring, until the pork is done, 7 to 10 minutes. Transfer to a large bowl.

Add the green onions, shallots, cilantro, mint, fish sauce, chili powder, and almost all the toasted rice, reserve some for sprinkling on top of the salad. Squeeze over the juice of a lime half. Stir to incorporate.

Taste the salad. It should be just a little hot, with some tartness from the lime juice with a nice taste of fish sauce. Add more fish sauce and/or lime juice as needed.

Separate the leaves of the lettuce. Divide the laab into the lettuce cups, top with the remaining toasted rice, and garnish with Thai basil.

THAI CUCUMBER SALAD

Serves 4 to 6

Sometimes the tastiest dishes are the simplest ones. Crunchy cucumber and shallots flavoured with garlic, lime and fish sauce. This is a great starter on its own or as a side dish with fish or seafood.

FOR THE DRESSING
1 clove garlic, finely chopped
1 small red bird's eye
    chili, seeds removed,
    finely chopped
1½ Tbsp (22.5 mL)
    fresh lime juice
1 Tbsp (15 mL) fish sauce
Pinch of granulated sugar
Pinch of salt

FOR THE SALAD
1 medium cucumber,
    cut diagonally into
    ¼-inch (6 mm) slices
3 shallots, cut into
    ¼-inch (6 mm) slices

For the dressing, whisk together all of the ingredients in a medium bowl until the sugar and salt are dissolved. Add the cucumbers and shallots and mix to combine.

TOM KA GAI
Serves 4

Coconut chicken soup, made citrusy by lime, lemongrass, and galangal. Galangal may look similar to ginger, but where ginger is hot, galangal is cool, and it has a refreshing, almost piney flavour. You don't need to peel it, but do just use the main part of the galangal and not any of the offshoots. You can also freeze galangal: cut it into coins, place separately on a baking sheet, and freeze; once frozen, transfer the coins into a freezer bag.

4 oz (110 g) skinless, boneless chicken thighs

1 stalk lemongrass

1-inch (2.5 cm) piece unpeeled galangal

4 lime leaves

2 red bird's eye chilies

2 cups (500 mL) coconut milk

1 cup (250 mL) water or chicken stock

2 Tbsp (30 mL) fresh lemon or lime juice

1 Tbsp (15 mL) fish sauce

¼ tsp (1 mL) finely grated or chopped palm sugar

¼ cup (60 mL) fresh cilantro leaves, to garnish

Slice the chicken into ¼-inch (6 mm) strips. Set aside.

Bruise the lemongrass by laying it on the cutting board and whacking on the surface with the dull side of a chef's knife. Cut into 2½-inch (6 cm) pieces. Cut the galangal into ⅛-inch (3 mm) slices, tear the lime leaves into thirds, and cut the chilies in half, removing the seeds. Set aside.

Bring the coconut milk and water (or stock) to a simmer in a medium saucepan over medium heat. Cook for 2 to 3 minutes, not letting it boil.

Reduce the heat to medium-low, and add the reserved lemongrass, galangal, lime leaves, and chilies. Cook for another 2 minutes, stirring constantly.

Add the chicken, and cook, stirring, for 5 minutes. Be careful not to overcook the chicken, and reduce the heat if the soup starts to boil.

Remove the pot from the heat. Stir in the lemon (or lime) juice, fish sauce, and sugar. Serve garnished with the cilantro.

HOT AND SOUR SOUP WITH SHREDDED CHICKEN AND LEMONGRASS

Serves 4

This soup is both spicy and sour and is a perfect example of how Thai dishes play on contrasting flavours. Chicken thighs work well in this recipe because they're meatier and have a deeper flavour than chicken breasts. Note the balance of flavours in the sweet palm sugar, tart lime juice, salty fish sauce, and spicy chilies. Add noodles and you've got Thai chicken soup!

2 stalks lemongrass, trimmed

4 cups (1 L) chicken stock

Pinch of finely grated or chopped palm sugar

4 slices unpeeled galangal

3 shallots, peeled

2 fresh lime leaves, torn, plus 5 leaves (centre vein removed), finely sliced

6 oz (170 g) skinless, boneless chicken thighs

3 Tbsp (45 mL) fresh lime juice, plus more to taste

3 Tbsp (45 mL) fish sauce, plus more to taste

4 red bird's eye chilies, bruised

3 Tbsp (45 mL) finely sliced lemongrass, to serve

2 Tbsp (30 mL) finely sliced shallots, to serve

2 Tbsp (30 mL) fresh cilantro leaves, for garnish

Bruise the lemongrass by laying it on the cutting board and whacking on the surface with the dull side of a chef's knife. Place the stock in a medium saucepan, and bring to a simmer over medium heat. Season with the pinch of palm sugar along with a pinch of salt.

Add the galangal, smashed lemongrass (kept whole), shallots, and torn lime leaves, and simmer for a few minutes. Add the chicken, and simmer until cooked, about 5 minutes.

Remove the pot from the heat, and transfer the chicken to a plate. Cover the stock. Let the chicken cool slightly, then coarsely tear or shred using your hands.

Strain the stock into another pot using a fine-mesh sieve, discarding the aromatics. Bring the stock to a simmer over medium heat.

Divide the lime juice, fish sauce, chilies (kept whole), and chicken meat into individual soup bowls. Pour over the hot stock. Add the sliced lemongrass, shallots, and sliced lime leaves. Check the seasoning; it should taste equally hot, sour, and salty. If necessary, adjust with more lime juice, fish sauce, and/or palm sugar. Serve sprinkled with cilantro.

THAI DUCK NOODLE SOUP

Serves 4 to 6

Here's a clever play on old-fashioned chicken noodle soup using the bones from our duck recipe on page 332. Cinnamon and star anise are go-to spices for duck, and the broth is perfumed with cilantro and garlic. The stock takes on a deep, rich colour, and the succulent flavour has a nice, sweet finish. There's a big difference between the taste, texture, and cooking time of vermicelli rice and egg noodles, so make sure you get the right ones. And the fried garlic—a common Thai garnish—is so delicious, you might just end up putting it on your cereal in the morning!

8 cups (2 L) chicken stock

Leftover bones from the
    Roasted Five-Spice Duck
    (page 332), and some of
    the leftover meat to serve

2 star anise

1 cinnamon stick, broken
    into small pieces

2 cloves garlic,
    coarsely crushed

4 cilantro roots,
    coarsely crushed

1 tsp (5 mL) black
    peppercorns

2 Tbsp (30 mL) soy sauce

1 tsp (5 mL) kecap manis
    (or Thai dark soy sauce/
    si-io dam)

1½ tsp (7.5 mL) finely grated
    or chopped palm sugar

1 tsp (5 mL) kosher salt

TO SERVE

11 oz (310 g) fresh or
    dried thin egg noodles,
    cooked (follow package
    instructions)

1 cup (250 mL) fresh
    bean sprouts

¼ cup (60 mL) finely sliced
    green onions

¼ cup deep-fried garlic
    (see below)

2 Tbsp (30 mL) red chili
    flakes (optional)

DEEP-FRIED GARLIC

Very thinly slice the garlic. Line a plate with paper towels. In a wok or a medium heavy-bottomed pot over medium-high, heat the oil until it reaches 350°F (177°C). Add the garlic, and gently stir until the garlic slices are fragrant, light brown, and crisp. Remove with a slotted spoon or spider, and drain on the paper towels.

In a stockpot or large saucepan, add the chicken stock and the duck bones. Bring to a boil over medium-high heat, then reduce to a simmer, cooking for 1 hour.

On a square of cheesecloth, pile the star anise, cinnamon, garlic, cilantro roots, and peppercorns. Gather into a pouch, and tie it together with some kitchen twine. Add the pouch to the stock, and simmer for another 15 minutes. Fish out the pouch and discard.

Season the stock with the 2 kinds of soy sauce, and the palm sugar and salt.

Divide the noodles, sliced duck, bean sprouts, green onions, and fried garlic among the serving bowls. Pour about 1 cup (250 mL) of the soup into each bowl. Season with chili flakes, if desired.

PORK SATAY
Makes 10-12 skewers

Classic Thai BBQ. Lemongrass, turmeric, and coconut milk—along with the other spices—elevate pork to a height that the humble hamburger can only dream of. If you're tired of the same-old when it's time to grill, these satays should become part of your outdoor cooking rotation.

1 pork tenderloin or loin,
    about 14 oz (400 g)
1 tsp (5 mL) coriander seeds
1 tsp (5 mL) cumin seeds
2 tsp (10 mL) white
    peppercorns
1 tsp (5 mL) roughly chopped
    unpeeled galangal
1 Tbsp (15 mL) roughly
    chopped lemongrass
1 tsp (5 mL) ground turmeric
1 cup (250 mL) coconut
    milk, divided
2 tsp (10 mL) finely grated
    or chopped palm sugar
1 tsp (5 mL) kosher salt
    or fish sauce
Peanut satay sauce
    (page 308)
10 to 12 bamboo skewers,
    6 to 7 inches (15–18 cm),
    soaked in cold water for
    15 minutes

Slice the pork into ⅜-inch-thick (1 cm) slices, and then into 3- by 1-inch (8 × 2.5 cm) pieces.

In a small skillet over medium-low heat, toast the coriander and cumin seeds until fragrant, 1 to 2 minutes. Let cool. In a spice grinder (or coffee grinder set aside for spices), process the coriander and cumin along with the peppercorns.

Using a mortar and pestle, pound the galangal and lemongrass into a paste. Transfer to a medium bowl. Add the turmeric, ground spices (coriander, cumin, and pepper), ½ cup (125 mL) of the coconut milk, palm sugar, and salt (or fish sauce), and mix well. Add the pork pieces and mix well. Cover and leave to marinate in the fridge for 30 minutes.

Preheat the grill to medium-high, then clean and oil the grill grates to prevent sticking. Pour the remaining ½ cup (125 mL) into a small bowl, and have ready a basting brush.

Thread the pork onto the soaked skewers, and place on a baking sheet. Grill the skewers, sliding a piece of aluminum foil under the exposed part of the skewers to prevent burning. Cook, turning the skewers and basting with coconut milk, for 5 to 8 minutes or until the pork is cooked through.

Serve with peanut satay sauce.

PEANUT SATAY SAUCE

Makes about 1½ cups (325 mL) satay sauce

This is the definitive sauce for satay drizzling and dipping. Roasted peanuts and sweet coconut milk get a boost from the sour tamarind and spicy curry paste. Use this sauce instead of ketchup the next time you serve up a quick Tuesday night chicken breast or pork chop. Make lots—it keeps in the fridge for about a week or so. See the recipe for the pork satay on page 307.

⅔ cup (160 mL) roasted peanuts
1 Tbsp (15 mL) vegetable oil
1 Tbsp (15 mL) Thai red curry paste (store-bought)
1 cup (250 mL) coconut milk
3 Tbsp (45 mL) finely grated or chopped palm sugar
½ tsp (2.5 mL) tamarind paste (page 312)

Grind the peanuts in a food processor until smooth.

Heat the oil in a wok or skillet over medium heat. Sauté the curry paste for 30 seconds, or until fragrant. Gradually add the coconut milk, stirring, and let simmer for 2 to 3 minutes. Add the peanuts, palm sugar, and tamarind paste. Continue simmering and stirring for 3 to 4 minutes, or until desired consistency.

PAD THAI
Serves 4 to 6

Probably the most-ordered dish at Thai restaurants in North America, and now you can make it at home. Preserved radish or turnip (*hua chai po*) is optional here, but it's worth looking for—it's that sweet, pickly note you taste in authentic pad thai. It's sold whole or already sliced. Garlic chives, also called Chinese chives, take on a lovely texture when cooked; substitute garlic scapes or green onions if you can't find them.

½ lb (220 g) dried
   wide rice noodles
5 Tbsp (75 mL) tamarind
   paste (page 312)
2 Tbsp (30 mL) fish sauce
1 Tbsp (15 mL) fresh
   lime juice
1 Tbsp (15 mL) finely grated
   or chopped palm sugar
4 oz (110 g) medium-firm tofu
   (about ½ cup/125 mL)
¼ cup (60 mL) vegetable oil
2 tsp (10 mL) chopped garlic
1 shallot, thinly sliced
8 large shrimp (10/12 count),
   peeled and deveined
3 Tbsp (45 mL) preserved
   radish, finely diced
   (optional)
1 large egg
1 cup (250 mL) fresh
   bean sprouts
2 Tbsp (30 mL) garlic chives,
   cut into 1-inch (2.5 cm)
   lengths
¼ cup roasted unsalted
   peanuts, finely chopped
¼ cup (60 mL) vegetable oil
Fresh sprigs of cilantro,
   for garnish
Lemon wedges, for garnish

Soak noodles in cold water for at least 1 hour, or until soft and pliable.

In a small bowl, mix together the tamarind paste, fish sauce, lime juice, and palm sugar. Set aside.

Cut the tofu into 1-inch (2.5 cm) cubes, and pat dry using paper towels. Line a plate with paper towels. Heat the ¼ cup (60 mL) oil in a wok over high heat, and cook the tofu until golden brown and slightly crispy on all sides. Remove the wok from heat, and using chopsticks or a slotted spoon, remove the tofu and let drain on the paper towels. Do not discard the oil in the wok.

Drain the noodles in a colander. Return the wok to the stove, and place over medium-high heat. Fry the egg without breaking, 1 to 2 minutes or until almost set. Turn it over and continue to cook without breaking.

Add the garlic, shallots, and shrimp, and the preserved radish (if using), and cook for 2 minutes or until the shrimp are cooked (they'll be opaque and crunchy). Set the shrimp and shallots to the side of the wok, and crack the egg right into the wok. After the bottom is set, break it up and incorporate it with the shrimp. Add the noodles, giving them a quick fold, and then the reserved tofu.

Add the tamarind sauce, and continue stirring and mixing for 1 to 2 minutes. Your noodles will have subsided to half their original volume.

Add the bean sprouts, garlic chives, and two-thirds of the peanuts. Mix together and let cook for another minute or so to heat it through.

Plate and garnish with the cilantro, lime wedges, and the remaining peanuts.

TAMARIND PASTE

Makes about 1½ cups (325 mL) tamarind paste

Tamarind provides the sour along with a bit of sweet to dishes. Several recipes throughout this chapter use tamarind paste, so make a large amount if you plan to make several Thai dishes in a week. Buy the tamarind that comes in blocks, and press the package to make sure it's soft. You can also start off by using tamarind sold without seeds; just reduce the water by half.

1 cup (250 mL) portion of packaged tamarind with seeds
1 cup (250 mL) warm water

Break up the tamarind with your hands or a knife, and place in a bowl. Cover with the water, and allow to sit for 10 minutes to soften. Using your hands or a spoon, mash up the tamarind.

Place in a fine-mesh sieve over a bowl. Using the back of a spoon, mash the fruit against the sieve to strain out any seeds or pods.

Keeps for 5 to 7 days in the fridge.

FRIED RICE WITH LYCHEE AND ROAST DUCK

Serves 2

Tired of Sunday night roast chicken? Whip up this elegant, knock-their-socks-off dish. The rich duck meat plays off the sweet lychee, all soaked up by fragrant rice. The recipe calls for a duck already roasted at your friendly neighbourhood Asian food store, so assembly couldn't be easier. This recipe features jasmine rice (named for the subtle, hunger-inducing aroma it gives off while being steamed). Use jasmine rice; no other rice will do when it comes to Thai food. Oh, and save the duck bones to make a delicious soup stock for our recipe on page 304.

¼ cup vegetable oil

2 cloves garlic, finely chopped

1 large egg

3½ oz (100 g) roast duck, finely shredded

2 Tbsp (30 mL) soy sauce

Pinch of ground white or black pepper, or to taste

2 cups (500 mL) cooked jasmine rice

1 tsp (5 mL) fish sauce

6 fresh lychee, peeled and pitted, or canned lychees, cut into ½-inch (1 cm) pieces

2 Tbsp (30 mL) thinly sliced green onions

10 to 12 snow peas, cleaned

1 Tbsp (15 mL) freshly chopped cilantro leaves

1 tsp (5 mL) finely grated or chopped palm sugar

1 tsp (5 mL) fish sauce

Lime wedges, for garnish

Fresh bean sprouts, to serve (optional)

1 Tbsp (15 mL) deep-fried shallots, for garnish (optional)

Heat the oil in a wok over medium-high. Fry the garlic briefly, or until fragrant. Immediately break the egg into the wok, and fry without moving until it's partially set, about 2 minutes.

Add the duck, and season with the soy sauce, white (or black) pepper, and a pinch of salt. Push the egg and duck to one side of the wok, and add the rice. Combine the 2 sides of the wok, mixing the rice, egg, and duck, by using a shovelling motion and working from the bottom up so that all the rice has a chance to fry in the oil. Do this for about 2 minutes.

Sprinkle more pepper on the rice, then add the lychees, green onions, snow peas, and cilantro. Add sugar and toss and for another minute, making sure the lychees are folded into the rice. Remove the wok from the heat, and sprinkle with the fish sauce.

Serve garnished with lime wedges, and with the bean sprouts and deep-fried shallots, if using.

PORK STIR-FRY WITH THAI BASIL AND FRIED EGG

Serves 2

Stir fries rock because they take only minutes to make. It's all about the right ingredients. In this dish, the lean pork plays nicely with the simple spices. Top the dish with fresh basil and fried eggs. As you eat, your chopsticks or fork pushes through the yolk, letting it run down and mix with what's underneath as the aroma of the pork wafts up to make you even hungrier.

1 tsp (15 mL) vegetable oil, for frying the eggs

2 large eggs

5 to 7 red bird's eye chilies, roughly chopped

3 cloves garlic, roughly chopped

1 Tbsp (15 mL) vegetable oil, for the stir-fry

3½ oz (100 g) pork tenderloin, cut into ⅛-inch (3 mm) slices

1 yardlong green bean, cut into ¾-inch (2 cm) lengths, or 10 to 12 snow peas)

1 tsp (5 mL) soy sauce

1 tsp (5 mL) granulated sugar

1 Tbsp (15 mL) oyster sauce

1 cup (250 mL) fresh Thai basil leaves

Freshly cracked black pepper, to taste

Steamed jasmine rice, to serve

In a small nonstick pan over medium-high heat, add the 1 teaspoon (5 mL) vegetable oil. Crack the eggs into the pan, and cook for 30 seconds or until partially set, and then reduce the heat to medium-low, cover, and cook until desired doneness. Set aside.

Pound the chilies and garlic together in a mortar and pestle. Heat the 1 tablespoon (15 mL) oil in a wok over medium heat, add the pounded chilies, and stir-fry for 1 minute or until fragrant. Add the pork and stir-fry for 3 minutes.

Add the beans (or snow peas), soy sauce, sugar, and oyster sauce, and stir-fry for about 1 minute. Add the basil leaves, stir-fry briefly, then remove the wok from the heat.

Arrange the stir-fry on a serving of jasmine rice, lay a fried egg on top of the pork, and finish with a crack of black pepper.

STIR-FRIED MUSHROOMS, BABY CORN, AND SHRIMP

Serves 4

There are more stir fries in Thai cuisine than pages in the longest cookbook. This one we chose because of its simplicity in preparation, appealing colours, and the prominent taste of oyster sauce. Oyster sauce is a thick, syrupy sauce made from cooking oysters down, and adding cornstarch, sugar, and salt. You can get it pretty much anywhere. You can also get fresh or frozen baby corn in all Asian grocery stores, and, in a pinch, the canned variety is usually available in larger supermarkets.

2 Tbsp (30 mL) vegetable oil

2 to 3 cloves garlic, finely chopped

8 to 10 large shrimp (10/12 count), peeled and deveined with tails left on

14 baby corn (fresh, frozen, or canned), sliced diagonally into 1¼-inch (3 cm) lengths

½ lb (220 g) snow peas (about 3 cups)

4 oz (110 g) cremini mushrooms, cut into ¼-inch (6 mm) slices

Fresh bean sprouts or pea shoots

2 green onions, cut into 1¼-inch (3 cm) lengths

2 Tbsp (30 mL) oyster sauce

1 tsp (5 mL) soy sauce

½ tsp (2.5 mL) superfine (caster) sugar or finely grated palm sugar

Heat the oil in a wok over medium-high. Stir-fry the garlic for 30 seconds or until fragrant. Add the shrimp, and stir-fry for 2 to 3 minutes or until almost cooked. Add the baby corn and snow peas to the wok, and stir-fry for 1 minute. Add the mushrooms, stir-frying for another 1 minute.

Add the bean sprouts (or pea shoots), green onions, oyster sauce, soy sauce, and sugar, and stir-fry for 30 seconds, or until the sauce is incorporated and all the ingredients are hot.

Serve with steamed jasmine rice.

TOFU STIR-FRY WITH BEAN SPROUTS
Serves 6

Tofu is an essential ingredient in most Asian cuisines, Thai food being no exception. Here we've chosen the extra-firm kind to stand up to being stir-fried with the garlic and bean sprouts (along with a bit of carrot for crunch and colour). There are many different types of tofu, all with different firmnesses and textures. It's very healthy, but the reason you want to try it more often is that its neutral flavour means it will work with whatever flavour combo you come up with.

1 cup (250 mL) vegetable oil

3½ oz (100 g) extra-firm
    tofu (about ½ cup), cut in
    ¾-inch (2 cm) dice

5 cloves garlic,
    finely chopped

1 cup (250 mL) carrot, cut
    into ¼-inch (6 mm) slices

3 cup (750 mL) fresh
    bean sprouts

3 red bird's eye chilies,
    sliced diagonally

2 green onions, cut into
    1¼-inch (3 cm) lengths

2 Tbsp (30 mL) oyster sauce

1 tsp (5 mL) soy sauce

Pat-dry the tofu using paper towels. Line a plate with more paper towels to drain the tofu after frying.

Heat the oil in a wok over medium heat. When it's hot, add the tofu, and stir-fry for 4 to 5 minutes or until golden. Remove with a slotted spoon or spider, and drain on the paper towels. Set aside.

Remove the wok from the heat. Set aside 2 tablespoons (30 mL) of the oil, then drain the rest from the wok (use for other dishes or discard).

Increase the heat to medium-high, and heat the reserved oil. Stir-fry the garlic and carrots for 1 to 2 minutes. Add the bean sprouts, and stir-fry for 1 minute. Add the chilies, green onions, the reserved tofu, and the oyster sauce and soy sauce, and stir-fry for another minute until all the ingredients are hot and mixed together well.

Serve with steamed jasmine rice.

JUNGLE CURRY WITH TROUT

Serves 4

This is called "jungle curry" because the abundance of green ingredients call to mind a jungle. This one is hot, folks, but you can turn down the heat by using fewer chilies. The complex flavour is achieved by including shrimp paste alongside the more traditional curry ingredients. Once you've chopped, diced, and made the paste, there aren't many steps to take. This is the key to great Thai food—thoughtful preparations in advance, allowing for quick cooking once you're ready to start. The French call this *mise-en-place*.

CURRY PASTE

10 to 15 green bird's eye chilies

3 Tbsp (45 mL) chopped shallots

2 Tbsp (30 mL) chopped lemongrass

2 Tbsp (30 mL) chopped garlic

1 Tbsp (15 mL) chopped unpeeled galangal

1 tsp (5 mL) chopped cilantro root

1 tsp (5 mL) freshly chopped lime leaves (remove centre vein before chopping)

1 tsp (5 mL) shrimp paste

Pinch of kosher salt or coarse sea salt

Garlic paste

2 cloves garlic

3 red bird's eye chilies, seeds removed

Crispy shallots

Vegetable oil for deep-frying, about 2 cups (500 mL)

6 shallots, cut into ¼-inch (6 mm) slices and slices separated

1 Tbsp (15 mL) all-purpose flour

FOR THE CURRY

Pinch of granulated sugar

1 Tbsp (15 mL) fish sauce

1 cup (250 mL) vegetable stock

10 baby canned corn, cut in half

12 to 15 snow peas

4 trout fillets, about 2 oz (60 g) each, skin on, scaled, and pin bones removed

2 Tbsp (30 mL) freshly chopped cilantro leaves

Fresh sprigs of cilantro, for garnish

. . . CONTINUED

CURRY PASTE: Place all of the ingredients in a mini food chopper, a food processor, or a mortar and pestle, and grind to a fine paste. If you're using a food chopper or food processor, you may have to add 1 to 2 tablespoons (15–30 mL) of water to help it purée. Set aside.

GARLIC PASTE: Pound the garlic, chilies, and a pinch of coarse sea salt in a mortar and pestle until smooth.

CRISPY SHALLOTS: Line a plate with paper towels. In a wok or a medium saucepan over medium-high heat, heat the oil to 350°F (177°C). On a plate, toss the shallots with the flour lightly just to coat. Deep-fry the shallots until golden and crispy, remove using a slotted spoon or spider. Drain on the paper towels. Drain the oil, and set aside 1 tablespoon (15 mL) for the curry. (Use the rest for another purpose.)

FOR THE CURRY: Heat the reserved 1 tablespoon (15 mL) oil from the deep-fried shallots in the wok over medium-high heat. Fry the garlic paste, stirring regularly until golden.

Add the curry paste, and fry until fragrant, about 1 to 2 minutes. Add the sugar, if using, and then the fish sauce. Add the stock and bring to a simmer, then add the corn, snow peas, and fish. Reduce the heat to medium-low (or a gentle simmer). Cook until the fish is just done, 1 to 2 minutes.

Finish with the crispy shallots and cilantro. Serve with steamed jasmine rice.

THAI YELLOW CURRY WITH VEGETABLES

Serves 6

There are many, many curries in Thai cuisine. As in India, every region, every valley, every home has its own special blend of ingredients and cooking technique. This is a vegetarian dish featuring yellow curry sauce, more mellow than its red or green counterparts. Thai eggplant is round and green; substitute Japanese eggplant if you can't find it.

YELLOW CURRY PASTE

2 tsp (10 mL) coriander seeds

2 tsp (10 mL) cumin seeds

1 tsp (5 mL) peppercorns

1 tsp (5 mL) ground turmeric

1 stalk lemongrass, tough outer leaves removed, chopped

1 medium Spanish onion, finely diced

2 red bird's eye chilies, seeds removed, roughly chopped

½-inch (1 cm) piece unpeeled galangal or peeled fresh ginger, roughly chopped

3 cloves garlic, roughly chopped

2 fresh lime leaves, finely chopped

FOR THE CURRY

2 Tbsp (30 mL) vegetable oil

1 cup (250 mL) coconut milk, divided

1 cup (250 mL) vegetable stock or water

1 tsp (5 mL) finely grated or chopped palm sugar

1 cup (250 mL) diced peeled carrots (medium dice)

8 to 10 baby canned corn, halved

1 medium red bell pepper, cut in medium dice

6 small Thai eggplants, sliced into ½-inch (1 cm) rounds

2 tsp (10 mL) soy sauce

15 fresh Thai basil leaves

YELLOW CURRY PASTE: In a spice grinder (or coffee grinder set aside for spices), grind the coriander, cumin, and peppercorns until it's a fine powder. Transfer to a food processor or blender along with the rest of the ingredients, and make a fine paste. You may need to add a bit of water or coconut oil to help the mixture purée.

FOR THE CURRY: In a wok or large skillet, heat the oil over medium heat. Add the curry paste, and sauté for 2 minutes, stirring constantly. Add ½ cup (125 mL) of the coconut milk, and cook for 2 more minutes. Add the stock (or water) and sugar, and season with some salt.

Add the carrots, canned corn, red peppers, and eggplants, and let simmer until almost soft but still slightly firm, about 3 minutes. Add the soy sauce, and the remaining ½ cup (125 mL) coconut milk.

Cover and cook for about 2 minutes. Remove the wok from the heat, and stir in the Thai basil.

Serve with steamed jasmine rice.

BEEF PANANG

Serves 6

There are many different types of curries in the Thai culinary repertoire. This is one of our favourites. Thai food is all about balance in flavour, aroma, and texture, and this dish has that balance in spades. Hearty beef short ribs are slowly braised in coconut milk infused with sweet sugar, salty fish sauce, and tangy kaffir lime leaves. The curry paste has deep complex flavours achieved by a few simple ingredients, including peanuts, chilies, coriander, and galangal. Think of galangal as a spicier ginger root; it's available in all Asian markets.

4 cups (1 L) coconut milk, plus 3 cups (750 mL) or more (optional)

3 lbs (1.4 kg) short ribs, cut into 2-inch (5 cm) bone-in chunks

1½ Tbsp (22.5 mL) finely grated or chopped palm sugar

2 Tbsp (30 mL) fish sauce

3 lime leaves, torn

2 red bell peppers, cut into ¼-inch (6 mm) slices

Large handful of fresh Thai basil leaves, about 1 cup (250 mL)

CURRY PASTE

7 dried long red chilies

¼ cup roasted peanuts

3 Tbsp (45 mL) chopped shallots

2 Tbsp (30 mL) chopped garlic

1½ Tbsp (22.5 mL) chopped peeled galangal

1 Tbsp (15 mL) chopped lemongrass

2 tsp (10 mL) chopped cilantro root

1 tsp (5 mL) cumin seeds

1 tsp (5 mL) coriander seeds

1 tsp (5 mL) kosher salt or coarse sea salt

. . . CONTINUED

Add the coconut milk to a large heavy-bottomed pot or Dutch oven, and bring to a boil over medium-high heat. Add the beef, then reduce the heat to a simmer, cover, and braise gently until fork tender, about 2 hours. Stir occasionally.

CURRY PASTE: While the short ribs cook, make the curry paste. Soak the chilies in a bowl of warm water until soft and pliable. Drain and discard the liquid. Cut open the chilies and remove the seeds.

Place the peanuts in a small saucepan, and cover with 4 inches (10 cm) of water. Bring to a boil over high heat, reduce the heat to low, and simmer for at least 30 minutes or until very soft. Drain and let cool.

In a mortar and pestle, pound the chilies and the rest of the ingredients for the curry paste except for the peanuts. Once ground, add the peanuts, and pound until you have a fine paste.

FOR THE CURRY: Once the short ribs are done, allow it to cool in the coconut milk, then remove and shred the meat from the bones, discarding the bones. Set aside the meat.

In a wok or medium saucepan, pour in either the coconut milk that the short ribs were cooked in or 3 fresh cups (750 mL) of coconut milk. (It's a matter of preference, depending on how meaty-tasting you would like the final curry.) Bring to a simmer over medium-high heat. Whisk in ¼ cup (60 mL) of the curry paste, reduce the heat to medium-low, and simmer for 10 minutes.

Add the palm sugar, fish sauce, and lime leaves, and simmer gently for 5 minutes. Add the reserved beef and the red pepper strips, and heat through. Remove the wok or saucepan from the heat.

Top the curry with a generous amount of Thai basil. Serve with steamed jasmine rice.

NOTE:
Curry paste keeps in the fridge for about two weeks. Try mixing a bit in your next BBQ marinade.

ROASTED FIVE-SPICE DUCK WITH PORT BERRY SAUCE

Serves 4

Here's a succulent duck dish that we're sure you'll make again and again. Five-spice powder—a combo of star anise, cloves, cinnamon, Sichuan pepper and fennel—is readily available everywhere. The brandy gives the glaze a punch, and the honey adds a sweet dimension that's perfect with duck meat. If you've ever roasted a chicken (of course you have . . . right?) then this is no more difficult. A great surprise for your next Sunday night family feast.

PORT BERRY SAUCE

1 cup (250 mL) port
½ cup (125 mL) frozen
   blackberries
½ shallot, chopped
2 tsp (10 mL) freshly
   chopped ginger
1 tsp (5 mL) black
   peppercorns
1 sprig fresh thyme

FOR THE DUCK

1 whole duck, about 2¼ lbs
   (1 kg), cleaned without
   giblets removed
¼ cup (60 mL) kosher salt
5 slices peeled fresh ginger
4 cloves garlic, chopped
3 to 4 cilantro roots, chopped
1 Tbsp (15 mL) brandy
1 Tbsp (15 mL) finely grated
   or chopped palm sugar or
   granulated sugar
1 tsp (5 mL) five-spice
   powder
1 tsp (5 mL) kosher salt
2 Tbsp (30 mL) honey
1 Tbsp (15 mL) soy sauce

PORT BERRY SAUCE: Place all of the ingredients in a saucepan, and bring to a simmer over medium-high heat. Reduce to a simmer, and cook for 15 minutes or until slightly thickened. Strain the sauce through a fine-mesh sieve, using the back of a spoon to mash through some of the pulp.

FOR THE DUCK: Preheat the oven to 300°F (150°C).

Rinse the duck well in cold water, and pat dry with paper towels. Rub the duck with the salt, and let stand for 30 minutes. Rinse off the salt in cold water, and again pat dry with paper towels. Set aside.

Pound the ginger, garlic, and cilantro roots in a mortar and pestle until smooth. Add the brandy, palm sugar (or granulated sugar), five-spice powder, and salt, and mix until combined. Rub the inside of the duck with this mixture, then place the duck on a roasting pan.

In a small bowl, mix the honey, soy sauce, and ⅓ cup (80 mL) of water. Brush the duck all over with this mixture, and repeat one or two times.

Roast the duck for about 1½ to 2 hours, or until the internal temperature reads 160°F (71°C), brushing the duck with the honey mixture every 30 minutes.

Remove the duck from the oven, cover with aluminum foil, and let rest for at least 15 minutes. First remove the drumsticks and wings, and transfer to a serving plate. Carve the rest of the duck, slicing into strips, and add to the serving plate.

Serve with the port berry sauce.

DEEP-FRIED SHRIMP IN TAMARIND SAUCE

Serves 3 to 4

Tamarind is a sour, tangy fruit common to Thailand and other Asian countries. It's important to Thai cuisine as it balances sweetness, heat, and saltiness. Tamarind pulp and paste are readily available in Asian markets and many larger supermarkets as well. This dish calls for jumbo shrimp that are deep fried for a few minutes without any breading or batter. Big shrimp hold up nicely in an oil bath and develop a wonderful colour and crispy exterior. Also, fried garlic is a common Thai garnish that's so delicious you might just end up putting it on your cereal in the morning!

TAMARIND SAUCE

3 Tbsp (45 mL) tamarind
   paste (page 312)
3 Tbsp (45 mL) palm sugar
   (chopped, pounded in a
   mortar and pestle, or
   finely grated) or
   granulated sugar
5 red and green bird's eye
   chilies, seeds removed,
   finely chopped
1½ tsp (7.5 mL) sriracha
   or other hot sauce
1½ tsp (7.5 mL) fish sauce
1 tsp (5 mL) oyster sauce
2 Tbsp (30 mL) water

FOR THE SHRIMP

Vegetable oil for deep-frying,
   about 3 cups (750 mL)
12 large shrimp (10/12 count),
   peeled and deveined
2 Tbsp (30 mL) deep-fried
   garlic (see the tip on
   page 304)
10 dried red chilies, crushed

For the tamarind sauce, combine all of the ingredients together in a small saucepan. Cook, stirring, over medium heat, for 3 to 4 minutes or until the mixture starts to become sticky. Remove the pan from the heat and set aside.

Line a large plate with paper towels. In a wok or heavy-bottomed pot over medium-high, heat the oil for deep-frying to 350°F (177°C). Pat the shrimp dry with paper towels.

Deep-fry the shrimp for 2 to 3 minutes, or until cooked. Remove with a slotted spoon or spider, and drain on the paper towels.

Reheat the tamarind sauce, then add the shrimp and mix well. Serve garnished with the fried garlic and dried chilies.

GRILLED BANANAS WITH SWEET STICKY RICE AND COCONUT

Serves 5

Sweet sticky rice with coconut milk makes a lovely Thai dessert, served with mango or any fresh fruit. Or try grilled banana, which gets all soft and smoky. While you're at it, why not add all the components of a traditional sundae? Sticky rice is also packaged as sweet rice or glutinous rice.

SWEET COCONUT STICKY RICE

2 cups (500 mL) white
    sticky rice
2 cups (500 mL)
    coconut milk
2 cups (500 mL) caster
    (superfine) sugar
2 tsp (10 mL) kosher salt

EQUIPMENT
Steamer basket

GRILLED BANANAS
5 ripe bananas or plantains
½ cup (125 mL) dried
    unsweetened
    coconut flakes
1 Tbsp (15 mL) granulated
    sugar

TO SERVE (OPTIONAL)
1 lime, cut into 5 wedges
Chocolate sauce (see below)
Coarsely chopped
    roasted peanuts
Lightly whipped cream
Vanilla ice cream

SWEET COCONUT STICKY RICE: Start soaking the rice the night before. Place the rice in a bowl. Working in the sink, add cold water to the bowl, and rinse the rice using your hands. Empty the bowl of most of the water, and repeat the rinsing and emptying a few more times. Finally, fill the bowl with cold water, leaving it overnight at room temperature.

The next day, drain the rice in a fine-mesh sieve, rinsing it with more cold water a final time. Cut a square piece of cheesecloth larger than your steamer basket. Lay it flat in the basket. Place the rice in the centre of the cheesecloth, then slightly flatten the mound of rice. (It won't cook evenly if piled too high in the centre.) Fold the overhang over the rice.

Bring a pot of water for the steamer to a boil, then add the steamer. Cover, reduce the heat to medium, and steam for 2 minutes. Reduce the heat to medium-low for an even gentler simmer. Steam the rice until tender, about 20 minutes, testing grains from the middle of the basket.

While the rice cooks, in a medium bowl, stir the coconut milk with the sugar and salt until they dissolve.

When the rice is done, transfer to a large bowl, and pour the coconut cream over the rice, stirring it in well. Cover and set aside in a warm place for at least 15 minutes before serving.

... CONTINUED

GRILLED BANANAS: Preheat a grill to medium-high, then clean the grill grates.

Using the tines of a fork, poke the bananas (or plantains) in a few places. Grill the bananas in their skin. When the skin begins to split, slit it open with a sharp knife so that steam can escape. Grill until the skin is charred and the inside is tender but still slightly firm, 4 to 5 minutes. Transfer the bananas to a plate.

In a small bowl, mix the coconut with the sugar. Add a pinch of salt. Sprinkle this mixture into where the banana is split.

Serve immediately with the coconut sticky rice. Eat by scooping out the banana and coconut together. If desired, before serving, squeeze lime juice over the banana, drizzle the plate with chocolate sauce, top with peanuts, etc.

EASY CHOCOLATE SAUCE

Chop enough semisweet chocolate to make 1 ¼ cups (310 mL) and place in a bowl. Place ¾ cup (185 mL) of heavy cream in a small saucepan over medium heat. Once it comes to a simmer, immediately pour it over the chopped chocolate. Add 1 tablespoon (15 mL) corn syrup, and cover for 10 minutes. Give the mixture another stir.

THAI MOJITO WITH LYCHEES

Serves 2

The cocktail you know and love but with sweet lychees and ginger.

½ cup (125 mL) fresh
   mint leaves

1-inch (2.5 cm) piece
   fresh ginger, peeled

Juice of 1 lime

¼ cup (60 mL) canned
   lychees in syrup

2 fluid oz (¼ cup/60 mL)
   light rum

½ cup (125 mL) soda water

Fresh sprigs of mint,
   for garnish

Muddle the fresh mint in the bottom of 2 serving glasses using a muddler or the end of a wooden spoon.

Very finely grate the ginger. To a martini shaker, add 2 teaspoons (10 mL) ginger along with the lime juice and a splash of the lychee syrup. Add the rum and soda water. Add a bunch of ice and shake to combine.

Add ice to the serving glasses, and pour the contents of the martini shaker over the ice. Garnish with lychees and sprigs of mint.

LIME LEAF AND WATERMELON MARTINI

Serves 6, and makes 2 cups (500 mL) infused vodka

We thought we'd have some fun with classic Thai ingredients in a not-so-common cocktail. Try it at your next party.

LIME LEAF—INFUSED VODKA
6 fresh lime leaves
2 cups (500 mL) vodka

FOR THE MARTINI
**1 cup (250 mL) chopped
  seeded watermelon**
Juice of 1 lime
**½ cup (125 mL) infused
  vodka**

Place the lime leaves and vodka in a jar, and let it sit, covered, for 5 days.

To a blender, add the watermelon, lime juice, and ½ cup (125 mL) of the infused vodka, and purée. Transfer to martini shaker with lots of ice, and shake.

Strain into martini glasses.

ABOUT THE HOSTS

From trendy restaurants in Buenos Aires to working with world-renowned chefs in New York City, award-winning chef **NATALIA MACHADO**'s profile has quickly earned international recognition. Born and raised in Buenos Aires, she spent summers in Patagonia, experiencing both big-city cuisine and the excellent seafood of the rustic coast. She's earned top honours and won television cook-offs, edging out the competition with her creativity and authentic Argentinean fare. Today, she is executive chef at Montreal's L'Atelier d'Argentine. Her biggest food vice is hot sauce.

Chef and instructor **VANESSA GIANFRANCESCO** has been cooking with her grandparents in Italy since she was two years old. Born and raised in Montreal by her northern Italian father and southern Italian mother, Vanessa believes Italian cooking is all about sharing, family, and togetherness. Her passion for food compelled her to leave law school to pursue a culinary career, and as a graduate of Montreal's Culinary Institute, she now teaches a pasta-making class. Cooking with V, her recently launched website, is dedicated to her mother and grandmothers, who taught her all there is to know about food. Her Sunday night go-to dinner is pizza, baked in her family's backyard wood-burning oven.

VIJAYA SELVARAJU is an adventurous and dynamic self-taught cook from Toronto. Born in Chennai, India, Vijaya and her family lived in Cameroon before moving to Canada. She's been making her mark on Canadian television since she was eight years old, appearing on *Video and Arcade Top 10*, *TVO Kids*, and as a guest panelist on *MTV Canada*. Today, she's the creator and host of Foodcapades, a popular YouTube web series that explores the culture and cuisine of the countries she visits. Vijaya thinks no dinner is complete without sauce, whether it's raita, mole, or creamy garlic tahini.

HANA ETSUKO DETHLEFSEN is passionate about simple and authentic Japanese home cooking. Born and raised in Canada to a Japanese mother and German father, Hana had the opportunity to live in Japan from 2001–2004. Her love of bridging culture and cuisine led to the creation of her cookbook, *Let's Cooking: A Go-To Guide on the Basics of Japanese Cuisine*, and her website. Today, Hana is a culinary arts instructor at the University of British Columbia and calls Vancouver home. Her favourite locally sourced dish is sea-inspired 親子丼 (*oyako donburi*)—grilled salmon and raw, marinated salmon roe on rice with mizuna greens.

PAILIN CHONGCHITNANT has always felt at home in the kitchen, and fondly recalls spending her childhood afternoons squeezing fresh coconut milk and grinding pork. Born and raised in Southern Thailand, she attended Le Cordon Bleu in San Francisco, and is the creator and host of Hot Thai Kitchen, a popular YouTube cooking show with an instructional approach. Pailin currently lives in Vancouver, where she's training to be a high school cooking teacher. If she had to choose one last meal, it would be her grandma's Hainanese chicken rice.

INDEX